THE WHOLE CRAFT OF
SPINNING

from the Raw Material to the
Finished Yarn

CAROL KROLL

Dover Publications, Inc.
New York

Preface

Today, there is renewed interest in spinning. Some people learn to spin primarily because they want to master the everyday crafts of our ancestors, and because they are fascinated by the tools and techniques which were used. For others, spinning provides a way to create unique and unusual yarns. They enjoy the experimentation with different fibers and color combinations, and the satisfaction that comes from making something new and exciting.

Whatever your reasons, spinning offers many rewards: the feel of the fiber in your hands, the rhythmic, relaxing movements and sounds of spinning, and especially the knowledge that you are making something that is truly your own, from the very beginning. While spinning is a highly creative craft, it is simple to learn, and therein lies both the fascination and the challenge.

C.E.K.

The Whole Craft of Spinning from the Raw Material to the Finished Yarn is a new work, first published by Dover Publications, Inc., in 1981.

International Standard Book Number: 0-486-23968-3
Library of Congress Catalog Card Number: 80-67835

Manufactured in the United States of America
Dover Publications, Inc.
31 East 2nd Street
Mineola, N.Y. 11501

Contents

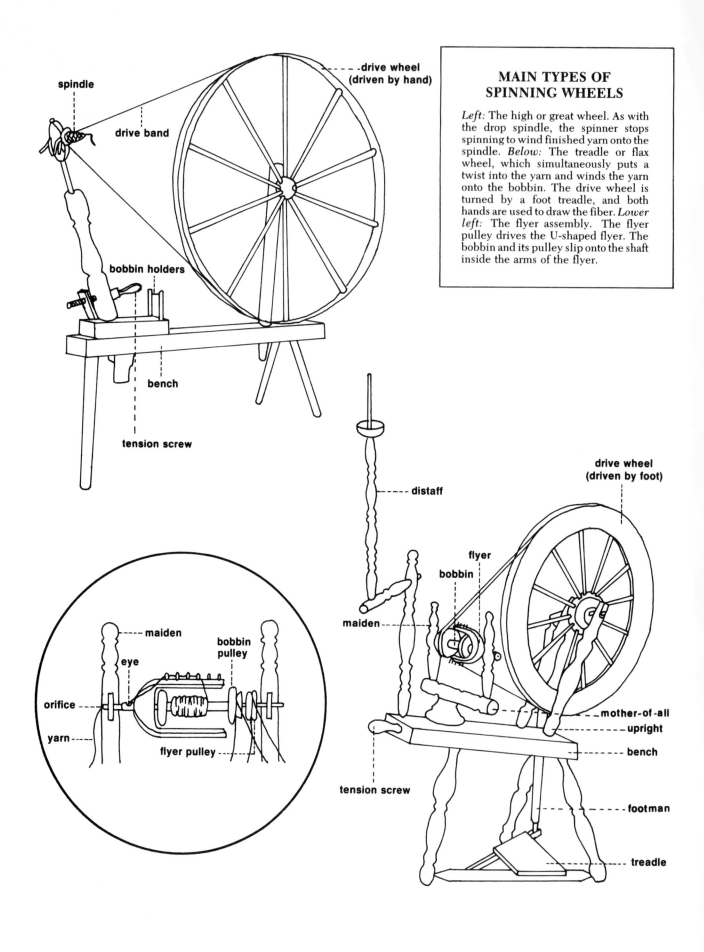

spindle

drive band

drive wheel
(driven by hand)

bobbin holders

bench

tension screw

**MAIN TYPES OF
SPINNING WHEELS**

Left: The high or great wheel. As with
the drop spindle, the spinner stops
spinning to wind finished yarn onto the
spindle. *Below:* The treadle or flax
wheel, which simultaneously puts a
twist into the yarn and winds the yarn
onto the bobbin. The drive wheel is
turned by a foot treadle, and both
hands are used to draw the fiber. *Lower
left:* The flyer assembly. The flyer
pulley drives the U-shaped flyer. The
bobbin and its pulley slip onto the shaft
inside the arms of the flyer.

distaff

drive wheel
(driven by foot)

flyer

bobbin

maiden

maiden

tension screw

mother-of-all

upright

bench

footman

treadle

bobbin
pulley

eye

orifice

yarn

flyer pulley

I

The Story of Spinning

The story of spinning is interwoven with the history of man. Paintings on Egyptian tombs record it. Grecian lyres and voices sing of it. Wherever any traces of early man have been found there has also been evidence of spun thread or spinning implements.

The first human attempts at spinning probably consisted of twisting animal fibers and suitable plant materials. The mere act of twisting them into strands made them useful and strong. The coarser fibers, such as jute or hemp, were usually used to make rope, cordage, and string, while finer ones, such as cotton, flax, silk, and wool, were used for cloth. Most early spinners were highly skilled craftsmen, despite the primitive tools which were used.

Many of the earliest spinning methods and tools described in this chapter are still in use today, especially the various drop spindles, and such types as the India and Navajo spindles.

EARLY HAND SPINNING

Some forms of hand spinning existed as early as twelve thousand years ago in North Africa, and fifteen thousand years ago in Asia. There were usually several basic methods: the yarn was either spun between the palms or fingers or it was spun using two hands and the thigh.

In the first method, the loose fiber was drawn out between the hands, twisted into yarn, then wound in whatever fashion seemed most satisfactory to the spinner. Often the yarn was wound around the center of a stick, or, less frequently, around the palm of one of the hands. Each step in the process—drawing, twisting, and winding—was done separately. It was therefore a three-step operation which was rather time-consuming.

In the second method, the fiber was usually drawn out by the left hand. Twisting was accomplished by rolling the right palm along the right thigh (assuming the person was right-handed). The newly spun yarn was then wound around a stick. This time the drawing and twisting occurred simultaneously; then the spinner stopped to wind the yarn—a two-step operation, and in that respect, an improvement over the finger or

palm method. In addition, the longer distance between the drawing hand and the thigh meant that more yarn could be spun at a time, and the thigh itself provided a sturdy base or platform upon which to work. This method is still employed by some spinners today.

HAND SPINDLES

Since early man often wound his yarn upon a stick, the next logical step was the use of this stick for spinning. By attaching the loose fiber or roving to the end of the stick and then rotating this stick, yarn could be spun. Thus evolved the hand spindle.

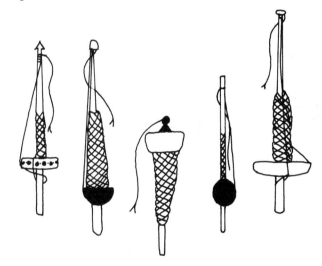

Hand or drop spindles.

Later, a weight, called a *whorl*, was mounted somewhere on the stick or *shaft*. When the shaft was rotated, the weight acted as a flywheel, both stretching and twisting the drawn-out fiber. At the top of some spindles, a notch or groove was carved to hold the yarn.

It is thought that the *distaff* was developed along with the spindle. This was simply a stick or rod used to hold the unspun fiber. Often this was pushed through the spinner's belt, or else held under one arm.

The Grasped Spindle

The grasped hand spindle was a New World innovation. This was a large hand spindle, with a shaft and a whorl, that was held in both hands and twirled in the air. Its spinning end and whorl were turned upward, away from the spinner, who simply grasped the lower end of the shaft. The fiber was first rolled into a rope-like, continuous roll or strand of fibers called a *roving*, then pulled through a suspended ring, or over a bar, above the spinner's head. This tension ring or bar held the roving back slightly, stretching it somewhat and drawing it out, while the spinner worked beneath it. As the fiber was pulled and lengthened, the spinner continued to roll the spindle between the hands with a tossing movement, twisting the roving into yarn. The yarn was then wound on the spindle shaft between the whorl and the spinner's hands.

In this method, the twisting and winding required the use of both hands, and the drawing, twisting, and winding were all done as separate steps. The yarn spun at one time by this method could be longer than yarn spun by other, earlier methods. On the other hand, the yarn was often more irregular, because the roving was not drawn out as evenly.

The Navajo and India Spindles

Navajo Indians used a large type of supported spindle that rested against the thigh as the spinner sat and worked. The left hand drew or *drafted* the fiber, while the spindle, rotated clockwise by strokes of the right hand, moved back and forth along the right thigh. Both hands were then used to wind the yarn on the shaft of the spindle. Drawing and twisting alternated with winding. Bedouin women and other early spinners used a similar method.

Another type of smaller supported spindle either stood erect on the ground or floor, or rested in a shell or wooden cup. The shaft and whorl were made of very light materials. One example of this type was the India spindle, which consisted of a delicate bamboo or iron shaft with a disc or ball of baked clay attached near its lower end to act as a whorl. This spindle was supported by resting it in the shell or cup, so that the weight of the spindle would not pull the thin yarns apart as they were being spun. Gossamer-fine strands could be spun as the spinner sat above, drawing fiber and twirling the spindle.

With the India spindle method, the yarn was twisted more firmly than with the larger Navajo variety. Both types produced a nice, uniform yarn and a more even spindle movement than was possible with the grasped spindle method.

The Drop Spindle

This type of spindle, suspended from the yarn it was spinning, rotated freely. The weight of the spindle stretched the roving after the left hand had drawn it out. The amount of fiber drawn was regulated by adjusting the spindle whorl, or weight.

The left hand held the fiber and drew it out, while the right hand alternately rotated the spindle and helped to regulate the twist as it ran up the strand. After the yarn was spun, it was wound on the right hand and then transferred to the shaft of the spindle. In an alternate twisting method, the palm of the right hand was rolled against the thigh, and the spindle was allowed to swing out as it twirled, giving it greater momentum.

A distaff was often used with the drop spindle, and it was common practice for a spinner to sit or walk about with the distaff held under one arm, or pushed through the belt.

There were many types of drop spindles. Most had a hook or cleft on the top of the shaft. Some had the whorl or a wooden crossbar near the top; others, near the bottom. On some types, yarn could be wound around spokes on the whorl, and the whole whorl could be removed.

With the drop spindle, there was greater momentum, because friction was reduced. The yarn was delicate, strong, and uniform. The twist was closer because the spindle moved so rapidly, and it was more regular because of the tension on the yarn. Sometimes yarns were respun for firmer twist, or else plied to make them heavier.

SPINNING WHEELS

The High Wheel or Great Wheel

The first true spinning wheel is believed to have evolved in India, anywhere from eight hundred to one thousand years ago. The idea spread to different parts of Asia and Europe, where diversity of design led to different types, and also different names, such as walking wheel, high wheel, wool wheel, and great wheel.

Arm-turned types were known to exist in parts of Germany in the thirteenth century, and in England by the fourteenth century. These early wheels were built on the principle of the supported spindle. A horizontally mounted shaft and whorl were turned by a large wheel. A driving band transmitted power to a pulley on the spindle. These wheels were used to spin flax as well as wool.

The spinner stood beside the wheel, often holding a wooden rod called a "spinner's helper" or "wheel finger" in her right hand. The roving

Spinning with a drop spindle.

Spinning flax on a Saxony wheel.

to be spun hung from the "spindle nib," or spindle tip. She turned the wheel clockwise with her right hand or the "wheel finger" and at the same time took several steps backward, while skillfully drawing out the fiber with her left hand. The wheel was twirled again, until the fiber was twisted sufficiently; then reversed for an instant, just long enough to unwind the yarn from the spindle tip. Now moving the wheel clockwise again, the spinner took a long step to the right so that the length of yarn was perpendicular to the spindle shaft. As the wheel continued to turn, the yarn wound around the base of the spindle. The spinner could then continue spinning by attaching a new strip of fiber to the end of the yarn she had just spun.

These early wheels provided a constant and even rotation, and the horizontal mounting of the spindle made the whole process easier, even though the spinner did have to stand and walk back and forth. Mechanical winding was also a great timesaver. Although the yarn output of these early wheels was not much greater than that of an accomplished spindle spinner, the early wool wheels did pave the way for later, more efficient types.

The Treadle Wheel or Flax Wheel

The treadle or flax wheel is thought to have evolved in the early part of the sixteenth century, although forerunners existed decades earlier. A treadle type was introduced in Brunswick, Germany, in 1533, by Johann Jürgen. This wheel had a flyer which put a twist into the yarn and a rotating bobbin which automatically wound the yarn. The flyer was a wishbone-shaped piece of wood, mounted on the shaft, and attached by a pulley to the drive wheel. The flyer—not the drive wheel—actually spun the yarn. Because the movement of the wheel could be controlled by the pressure of the foot on the treadle, the spinner had both hands free to draft the fiber. Another advantage was that she could sit. All three spinning processes could be carried on at one time, with very little effort. Greater speed and increased production were possible.

Although there are plans for a crank-operated flyer mechanism in the drawings of Leonardo da Vinci, and there were earlier experiments with "flyer-wheels," it was Johann Jürgen who actually introduced the flyer and bobbin assembly. It is his wheel upon which all later spinning wheels with flyer mechanisms are based.

Treadle wheels were used for spinning a variety of fibers. Wheel names varied—Saxony, Brunswick, Norwegian, Old Dutch, Irish, Russian, etc. Wheel and bench designs varied, too. Some had the spindle supported on just one end, others on both ends; some had a drive wheel with just one band to the spindle and only one pulley instead of two. Although the majority of wheels had one long, continuous driving band, which ran from the large wheel to two pulleys, crossing once, some wheels had two separate driving bands.

Treadle wheels also had distaffs, which were either attached to the wheels themselves, or placed on stands next to the wheels. When the wheel was used for spinning flax, the distaffs were dressed with the flax for ease in spinning. Wool spinners usually did not use the distaff, but placed the carded wool in a basket instead.

The majority of treadle wheels were of the "Saxony type," with the wheel to the right side of the spinning mechanism, and the treadle beneath the drive wheel. "Parlor wheels," or upright types, were also popular. These handsome and beautiful wheels took up less space because the spinning apparatus was mounted above the drive wheel, which in turn was mounted above the bench and treadle. The parlor wheel was also known as the "German wheel" or "cottage wheel." On later models there were sometimes two bobbin and flyer units, that could be used by one or two spinners. These were known as "gossip wheels" or "lover's wheels."

Chair wheels were another variation. Four legs supported the large wheel and the spinning assembly. Sometimes there was also a second, small acceleration wheel. Many of these chair wheels had two treadles. Some had only one pulley located on the bobbin. The spindle and flyer were turned by the drag of the yarn as it wound on the bobbin.

As modern machinery took over the tasks of spinning and weaving, most of the lovely old wheels disappeared from parlors and kitchens, and were either discarded or stored in attics and sheds. Today, some of these treasured pieces have found their way back into museums and homes; most stand as silent reminders of our past, but a few are being used once again by the spinners of today.

II
Preparing the Fiber for Spinning

Before you can begin spinning, some care must be taken in selecting and preparing the fiber. Before a fiber can be spun into yarn, it often needs to be sorted or picked over, and possibly cleaned, teased, and carded so that it is free of lumps and tangles, as well as bits of dirt and straw. Careful preparation will result in easy spinning and a durable, high-quality yarn.

SELECTING THE FIBER

It will be much easier to learn how to spin if you use wool for your first attempts at spinning. Most of the instructions and techniques described in this chapter, therefore, pertain to working with wool. Once you have become skilled at spinning, you may wish to experiment with other fibers, some of which require a little more ability and experience. These techniques are described in greater detail in chapters seven and eight.

Wool grows in locks. Each lock is made up of many single fibers, and these have tiny scales on their outer surfaces, microscopic projections which overlap, pointing toward the tip of the fiber. Because of these scales, wool has a tendency to felt, or mat, when improperly handled. Sudden exposure to very hot or very cold water, steam, or even excessive handling when the wool is wet can cause this. The wool fibers actually interlock. While this felting quality is usually a liability to spinners, manufacturers often consider it an asset. They layer carded wool, and subject it to both steam and pressure. Then they put the wool through an acid bath and pound it. The finished product—felt—is used in hats and coats, as well as for many other purposes.

There are a few things you should know about sheep and wool. Sheep are given a blood grade, described in terms such as "full-blood," "half-blood," "quarter-blood," "eighth-blood," and "braid." These terms refer to how much fine-wool blood is in the breeding. The higher the blood grade, the finer the wool. Full-blood or half-blood would be quite fine; braid would be coarse.

Spinning count is another term you'll encounter. It is a numerical system based upon the number of 560-yard skeins of yarn that can be spun from a pound of wool. Spinning count is expressed in terms such as "50s" or "64s." The higher the number, the finer the wool.

Basically, there are three categories when it comes to sheep—fine-wool, cross-breeds, and mutton breeds. The fine-wools include Merino and Rambouillet, and have a spinning count in the 60s to 100s range. They are extremely soft and fine, with a short staple length of 2" or 3", and are very tightly crimped, or waved. Wool from these types is excellent, and especially nice for fine knitting yarns.

Cross-breeds include such types as Columbia, Corriedale, and Targhee. This wool has a spinning count in the 40s to 58s range, with a staple length of about 2" to 5". The fibers are silky and easy to handle. This kind would be a good choice for those learning to spin.

The mutton breeds can be further divided into medium-wool and long-wool varieties. Included in the medium-wool class would be breeds such as Cheviot, Dorset Horn, Hampshire, Shropshire, Southdown, and Suffolk. These have spinning counts in the 50s to 60s range, and a staple length of from 2" to 5". They are easy to spin, and fine enough to make very nice yarns for a multitude of uses.

Long-wools include such types as Cotswold, Lincoln, and Romney. The wool has a spinning count anywhere from 28s to around 48s, and the staple length varies from about 7" to 12"—sometimes more. The wool tends to be coarse and wavy, or widely crimped, and is suitable for durable worsted yarns. The Karakul sheep also produces a fairly long, coarse coat. As these sheep grow older, the black or dark wool is covered with a protective coat of coarse grayish hair. Yarns spun from Karakul have an interesting texture and can be quite attractive. The fleece is darker and of better quality when shorn from a fairly young sheep. Fleece from the older Karakul is more easily spun when blended with the white wool of another breed. The result is a very pretty, textured gray yarn.

Until you are more familiar with the various breeds of sheep, and the different types of wool, your best bet is to purchase your wool from a spinning supply house, a shop, or a wool cooperative that sells wool to spinners. That way you're more likely to obtain high quality fleece. If possible, buy "grease wool," which is wool that has been recently shorn and still has the natural lanolin or "yolk" in it. You'll find "grease wool" easier to spin.

The quality of the wool varies according to breed, but also according to how well the sheep were cared for, and the area in which they were raised. Try to examine samples before you buy. For your first attempts, avoid purchasing wool that is either very short and fine or very long and coarse. A staple length of 3″ to 5″ is easiest to handle. If you are buying wool in fleece or lock form, the locks should be strong. They should not break when held at both ends and given a good, healthy tug. The wool should also be unmatted and relatively clean. If it's very dirty, you'll be paying for the dirt as well as the wool, since the wool is sold by the pound. In addition, if the wool is reasonably clean, you may not have to wash it at all before spinning.

If you buy wool in a long, rope-like roving, often called "wool top," ask for a medium grade. If spinning count is given, ask for something in the 48s to 60s range. Usually when you buy wool top, you aren't able to learn what type (or types) of sheep the wool came from. It's often a mixture of breeds, and the wool will be scoured and combed. Wool tops and rovings, however, are nice and clean, and there is no waste. When you become more proficient at the craft, you may want to try spinning some of the various fibers available in roving form.

Most spinners seem to have a preference for either raw wool—right from the sheep—or scoured wool, which has been washed. Some advantages of using raw wool are that you can get a sampling of various breeds, and sometimes some very lovely color variations. In addition, if you plan to blend the wool with something else, the greasy lanolin helps hold the other fiber.

An advantage of having scoured wool is that there is less work—a real time-saver. This can be a money-saver also because there is no weight loss due to lanolin and dirt. Scoured wool is available in many forms—wool top, rolags, even pencil-thin roving ready to spin.

It's sometimes fun to buy wool from a neighbor who raises sheep. Be sure, though, that the lanolin is still soft, and that the wool is reasonably clean. Don't buy "second cuts," which are short bits of wool, cut on both ends. This is wool that the shearer had to go back and clip more closely. Ask the owner of the sheep to remove the stiff and really dirty, blackened outer edges of the fleece before weighing it. There's no reason to pay for something that is unusable. (Don't throw out wool that is simply lanolin-stained but otherwise clean; the stain will wash out easily.) Be certain that the locks are unmatted and strong. After you have spun the yarn, you might want to show the owner how it turned out.

Some spinners feel that by buying a sheep or two, or a small flock, they will be assured of all the wool they might need. Sheep raising is a wonderful hobby or business, but it is not for everyone. Each year there are sheep for sale simply because someone did not have the time or knowledge to raise them properly. Unless you have the resources, you'd probably be just as wise to buy your wool from a wool cooperative, a craft shop, or a spinning supply house. That way, you'll also have a variety of types and colors from which to choose, and you can purchase the wool in any form you desire—a fleece, clean grease-wool, or scoured, and carded or combed.

If you are seriously considering sheep raising, there are several good books available for spinners who want to raise a small flock of their own. See "Sources of Supply" at the end of this book.

There are so many types of wool available, and you'll enjoy experimenting with them. In time you'll learn which will give you fine woolen yarns, and which will give you durable worsteds. You'll make your choice according to how you intend to use your yarn.

SORTING

Someday, you may want to buy raw wool, in fleece form, right off the sheep. A really good fleece is quite uniform all over, in terms of the length and texture of the wool, except for the legs, haunches, and tail areas. Most fleeces, however, will have more variation, and you will need to sort the wool.

Your fleece may be tied with a band of neck wool (or neck, tail, and leg wool together), or it may be tied with twine. Spread the wool out on newspaper, and begin picking it over, dividing it into piles according to variations in texture, waviness, length, and color. As you sort, work from the outer edges of the fleece toward the center. I usually throw away the very dirty parts from the outer edge of the fleece.

As you work inward, you'll find wool from the neck, belly and head. It is shorter than the wool in the center, and often quite fine. Save this for making some of the novelty yarns that call for adding bits and pieces. You will also find coarser wool from the hind legs and haunches. This is good wool for heavier, bulky yarns. Last, you will have the longer, softer wool from the shoulders, back, and upper sides. This is the best wool. As you sort the locks, gently spread or pick them apart with your fingers, shaking them over the newspaper to remove as much dirt or unwanted matter as possible.

Sorting is usually necessary. If you don't do it, noticeable irregularities may show up in your yarn. The various types also take dyes differently; coarse wools usually take dyes less readily than fine ones.

Other types of fibers may also need sorting—fur or hair, for example. Divide them into groups according to length, texture, and color before working with them further. More detailed information on working with other fibers is given in chapters six and seven.

WASHING

Often you will be using wool that is clean enough not to need washing or scouring until after you've spun it. But if you want to remove some or all of the dirt before spinning, go ahead. Sometimes the lanolin in the wool has hardened, and if that's the case, it's always best to wash and re-oil before carding and spinning. The main thing to remember is that you should wash very *gently*, handling the wool as little as possible, and that the wool should not be subjected to very hot or very cold water—*no extremes in temperature.*

Steep the wool in several soap and water baths. Use soft, lukewarm water, and either soap or a mild detergent, such as that used for washing dishes. I prefer soap flakes, unless I plan to dye the wool later, in which case I use a detergent in order to remove all grease more effectively. If you dye fiber with traces of grease in it, the dye won't take evenly.

Add some salt to the first soap bath—about half as much salt as there is soap or detergent. Then put the wool in, letting it sink to the bottom by itself. You can help it along a little by pressing it down gently until the fiber is submerged. Let the wool soak for awhile—at least 15 minutes. The water will become very dirty. After soaking, lift the wool out gently, being careful not to stretch or twist it.

Put the wool in several more lukewarm soapy baths, without the salt this time, until it is clean. Then soak it in several lukewarm rinse baths, press the water out gently, and drain in a colander or dish drainer. Transfer the wool to a fluffy towel, and blot it to remove excess moisture. Place the wool on a rustproof screen to dry in a shady place away from excessive heat.

If you want to remove the dirt and leave some of the natural lanolin in for spinning, use cool water instead, and no soap. Just let it soak for awhile. Don't use a substance such as "Woolite," because it does remove the lanolin from the wool. Some people, by the way, prefer to leave part of the lanolin in even after spinning because yarns of this type have a high degree of natural water-repellency. When articles of clothing made of these yarns become damp, there is a slight odor, which is agreeable enough to some, and disagreeable to others. Actually, even when the lanolin has been completely removed, wool doesn't absorb water easily.

Occasionally, but not often, the wool is so dirty or greasy that ordinary washing is not enough. In that case, gradually bring a detergent and water bath to a simmer, after immersing the fiber first. Don't let it boil; just simmer it for about 50 minutes or so. Then let it cool, and rinse it in water that is the same temperature as the cooling bath. Dry in the shade.

Other animal fibers, such as fur or hair, should probably be washed unless they are from a pet who is quite clean, or unless you purchased the fiber, already clean, from a shop or spinning supply house that sells to spinners.

If you obtain some very dirty or "fragrant" combings or clippings from any animal—dog, goat, rabbit, or whatever—don't throw them away until you've tried washing them first. Some spinners feel that washing removes all the natural oils, and that spinning will be difficult. Don't believe it. Many animals don't have that much natural oil in their fur or hair. In most cases, you'd have to add additional oil before spinning it anyway. So if it is dirty, and you'd like to work with it clean, go ahead and wash it. Just handle it gently, as you would wool. Most fur and hair will require less soaking time than wool. Some types of fur will mat, just as wool will, but most hair will not. Hair does have a tendency to tangle, however, if you agitate it too much.

The best way I've found to wash hair or fur is to pack it very loosely, after sorting, in bags made from old nylon stockings. This keeps the fibers together, so that they don't line the sink or clog the drain. Then steep the bags of fiber in several lukewarm detergent and water baths, and several lukewarm rinse baths. Place the wet bags on a towel, and blot to remove excess water. Remove the fiber and spread it out to dry on a flat surface, preferably a rustproof screen that allows air circulation for faster drying. As the fiber dries, gently tease it apart with your fingers.

If you're worried about removing the odor from some very dirty fiber, use a cleaning agent that really dissolves animal oils. Some spinners use dog shampoo for this purpose. If all else fails, put the fiber in a detergent and water bath, and gradually bring it to a simmer. Keep it simmering (not boiling) for about half an hour. Then cool, and rinse in water about the same temperature as that in which the fiber has cooled.

Adding a fabric softener or hair conditioner to the final rinse bath will improve both the appearance and the feel of the yarn.

Most vegetable fibers can be purchased after they have been already cleaned, and ready to card or spin. A few—such as silk or cotton—may need special treatment, depending upon what state they are in when you buy them. If you can't buy them already cleaned, refer to the fiber in question in chapter seven. You'll find more specific information there.

ADDING OIL

Spinning oil can be added to animal fibers prior to carding and spinning, to make the job easier. Some spinners feel that all animal fibers should be heavily oiled, or greasy. Others use very little spinning oil, or none at all. I often spin scoured wool without any added lubricant, but I usually add oil when working with very fine, short, or delicate fibers, such as pet fur. Again, it's a matter of personal preference.

You can purchase spinning oils, or make your own. A friend of mine uses neat's foot oil mixed with washing soda and water. She combines ¼ cup of the soda with four cups of water, then adds enough oil to make it as slippery as she likes. Lanolin, olive oil, or mineral oil are also good choices. Baby oil, which usually contains mineral oil, or both mineral oil and lanolin in a form that does not become rancid, can also be used.

Spread the fiber on newspaper, and sprinkle the oil over it. Then gently work the oil into the fiber with your fingers. Use enough oil to make spinning easier, but not so much that the fiber feels slick and sticks to your fingers. When the oil is fairly well worked in, place the fiber in a paper bag or cardboard box, or even a basket—nothing airtight. Cover it loosely. I usually place several folded newspapers or a cloth on top of the container, unless it is a paper bag, which can simply be closed. Let the oiled fiber sit overnight, and by morning the oil will have completely penetrated the fiber.

When I plan to card fur or hair, I often add a little water to home-made spinning oils (about one part water to one part oil). Then I shake the oil and water to form an emulsion, and sprinkle it on the fiber. The addition of water prevents any buildup of static electricity that might occur when the fiber—especially the more flyaway types; such as pet hair or angora—is carded. There is nothing quite as irritating as having fur or hair all over you, clinging to your arms, lap, and face. Adding water eliminates this problem. If you buy a commercial spinning oil, you may find that accompanying directions for use call for the addition of some water.

Vegetable fibers are usually dampened with water or spun dry, depending upon the type. Yarn or thread that is spun wet will be smoother than that which is spun dry.

CARDING

Before the cleaned and oiled fibers can be drawn out and spun into yarn, they usually require some further preparation. Some need only a gentle teasing with the fingers prior to spinning, but most fibers will require carding. When you card the fiber, you straighten and dress it, forming a roll or batt that is even in texture, and free of lumps and tangles. When carding is done properly, spinning is smooth and effortless.

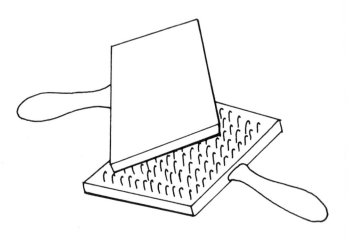

Carding combs.

If you are planning to do any amount of spinning, you should invest in a pair of carding combs or "carders." Carders are simply a pair of paddles, usually rectangular in shape, with handles attached. Each carder is covered on one side by little bent wire teeth, pitched at an angle. These teeth are embedded in a backing of some sort, often leather or cloth. There are many types of carders. Some spinners prefer wooden ones, since they are lighter. Others prefer the heavier metal ones because they are more durable. Carders are also available in both flat-back or curved-back styles. I prefer the flat-backed ones because of the strong, flat surface they provide for carding. But others like curved backs, and I suppose it's largely a matter of what you become accustomed to. Size is another factor to consider. If you buy carders that are very small, they won't hold as much fiber; it's wiser in the long run to buy ones with a carding surface that measures at least 4½″ × 8½″.

You'll learn, too, that there are carders with large, widely spaced teeth, and carders with small, fine, closely spaced ones. The ones with larger, widely spaced teeth are better for working with fiber that is coarse, tangled, or lumpy. Carders with fine, closely set teeth are better for fiber that has already been carded once, but needs further carding, or for fibers that are very delicate, such as furry or downy ones. The best all-around choice for a beginner is a pair of medium gauge wool carders, number 9 or 10. These are adequate for most purposes.

If you have some old carding combs, you may still be able to use them. If there aren't any missing teeth, and they are still embedded firmly in the backing, they're probably fine. I found a pair like this. The only thing wrong was that the teeth were dull. I took a sharpening stone—the type used to sharpen knives—and stroked the teeth from top to bottom several times. Then I stroked from bottom to top until the teeth had been sharpened enough to do a good job of carding. You can do this with the newer cards too when they become dull.

If the teeth on an old carder are very loose, or falling out, or if they are too worn, you can sometimes buy another piece of card clothing with new teeth. Some companies will send you replacement clothing; others will not. If you can get the card clothing, remove the old clothing and tack on the new. The backing and teeth on some new carders can also be replaced. It depends upon the manufacturer. Refer to the "Sources of Supply" section at the end of this book.

If you plan to spin long fibers, ones that are really too long to handle on regular carding combs, you should have a long-toothed metal comb (such as a dog comb) or a flicker comb on hand. A flicker comb is simply a small carder that is used for "flicking" or spreading longer types of hair or wool so that the fibers are easier to draw for spinning.

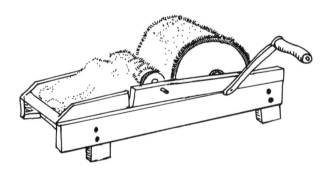

One type of cylinder carding machine.

For the spinner who has very large amounts of fiber to card, crank-operated cylinder carding machines are also available. The carding surfaces are attached to two cylindrical drums, which rotate when the crank is turned. The fiber is fed under the smaller drum and is automatically spread on the larger drum. The batt is then pulled off by hand. Carding machines may have either a wood or metal frame, and some models are more efficient than others. Complete directions come with the machines.

The fiber may be prepared by either the woolen or worsted method, depending upon whether you want a loose, soft yarn or a firm, more tightly twisted one. *A woolen yarn* is fluffier and more loosely twisted, with a characteristic bounciness. There are a large number of fiber tips on the surface of the yarn, giving it a downy or fuzzy appearance. Shorter and finer fibers are most often spun by the woolen method.

Carded fiber, woolen method.

Carded fiber, worsted method.

A *worsted yarn* is durable, firmer, and more tightly twisted. The fibers are combed differently, so that any short ones are removed, and the remaining long ones are left in a parallel arrangement. Longer fibers are usually spun by the worsted method.

To prepare the fiber for woolen spinning, hand carders are required. The fiber is placed on the carders, brushed, then removed in the form of a batt. The batt is then shaped into a little roll, called a rolag, which has an even density throughout, and is loose and fluffy. The individual fibers run in several different directions. A fiber for worsted spinning can be prepared with carding combs, by handling the fiber differently, or by drawing the fiber through long-toothed combs. Both methods are explained in detail below.

When you obtain your cards, or carders, mark one "L" for the left hand, and the other "R" for the right one. Then always use each in the proper hand. When you have finished working with your cards, store them in the open air. If you keep some greasy or oily wool between them, they won't rust, and they'll last for many years. In addition the backing will last longer.

The Woolen Method

Sit comfortably on a chair. Put on an apron, or else drape a towel across your lap. Put some finger-teased wool on the carder marked "L," with the strips of fiber running vertically.

Step 1: Place the left-hand carder on your lap, teeth up, handle pointing away from you. Grasp the handle with your left hand, fingers up. Take the other carder in your right hand, teeth down, and begin to comb the fiber on the left-hand card. Pull the top card through very lightly, stroking several times, until the fibers become well-distributed.

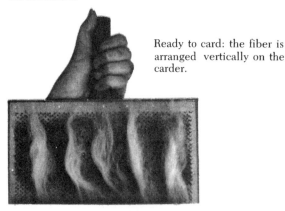

Ready to card: the fiber is arranged vertically on the carder.

Step 2: Now transfer the wool to the right-hand carder. Place the left-hand carder above the right, so that the teeth are together and the handles point toward you. Place the top edge of the right-hand carder against the top edge of the left, and draw the right-hand one, which is on the *bottom*, toward you, pressing gently as you strip the left-hand carder of fiber in several short strokes. All the wool will now be on the right-hand carder.

Carding the fiber.

Step 3: Repeat Step 1.
Step 4: Transfer the wool to the left-hand carder. Again place the left-hand carder above the

right, teeth together and handles pointing toward you. But this time, draw the left-hand carder, which is the *top* one, over the right-hand carder, in several short, light strokes. Pull toward you. All the wool will be transferred to the left-hand carder.

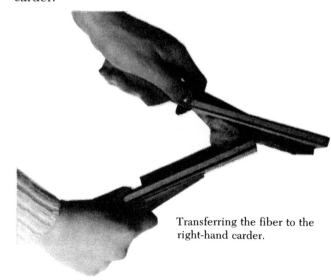

Transferring the fiber to the right-hand carder.

Step 5: Repeat Step 1.
At this point the wool may be carded sufficiently, but if not, continue to alternately comb and transfer the wool, back and forth, until the fibers lie straight, and tangles are removed.

When you are ready to remove the batt from the carders, strip the wool from the left-hand carder with the top edge of the right, as in Step 2. Then strip the wool from the right-hand carder with the top edge of the left, as in Step 4. Use short, lifting strokes. The wool will lie in a roll across the top of the left-hand card when you're finished, and you can remove it with your fingers. This batt or roll is called a *rolag*, and from this rolag you will spin your woolen yarn.

Transferring the fiber to the left-hand carder.

If you are working with very heavy or lumpy wool, you may have to card it more than once, beginning with carders that have large, widely spaced teeth, and finishing with carders that have shorter, closely set ones.

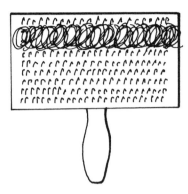

When carding is completed, the fiber lies in a roll across the top of the left-hand carder.

When carding hair or fur, it's usually not necessary to transfer the fiber from one carder to the other. In most cases, just one "comb-through" is enough to straighten the fibers sufficiently. Use very light pressure on the carders. If you have added enough oil to the fiber, the rolag will hold together very well.

The Worsted Method

Arrange the long fibers vertically on the left-hand card, and stroke with the right, just as in the woolen method. However, when it's time to remove the fiber, use your fingers and roll the fibers off across the *width* of the card instead of the *length* as in the woolen method. This will leave the fibers in a parallel arrangement and in a nice, neat bundle for worsted spinning.

Another way to prepare the fiber for worsted spinning is to draw a small, single carder, called a "flicker," through the locks of wool or hair. This loosens and straightens them and works well if the fibers are all about the same length. The easiest way to do this is to hold the fiber tips in one hand and comb through with the other, toward

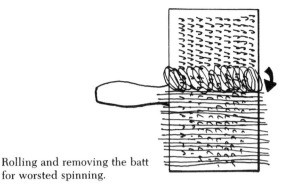

Rolling and removing the batt for worsted spinning.

the open end of the lock or bunch of hair. It's a good idea to work on a board placed upon your lap. If hair fibers vary in length, and you want to remove the shorter ones, use a comb with metal teeth, such as a dog comb. The long fibers will be left in a parallel arrangement, and the shorter ones will be left in the teeth of the comb. (These shorter lengths of hair could later be carded for woolen spinning, perhaps combined with another fiber.)

The thickness of the rolags will vary according to the fiber being used, and how cohesive it is. Generally, for wool, the rolag should be anywhere from 1″ to 2″ thick. If the fiber holds together well, the rolag can be thinner than when you are working with short or slick fibers. I often work with a 2″ or 2½″ rolag when the fiber is more difficult to control, and I oil it heavily enough so that it holds together well. Experience will show what works best.

For thinner yarn, such as a worsted with a tight twist, you can draw the rolag out a bit more by pulling it gently lengthwise with your fingers. The lengths of this roving can then be arranged horizontally on your lap, ends overlapping, when you are ready to spin. Rolags for woolen spinning can also be stacked upon your lap before spinning so that spinning is more continuous. Once you become adept, you'll find that you won't have to stop very often if you handle the rolags in this manner.

III

Spinning with the Drop Spindle

You really don't have to own a spinning wheel in order to spin your own yarns; a simple drop spindle will suffice. In fact, it's actually a good idea to learn to spin on a drop spindle first, even if you own a wheel. Spinning on the wheel is more easily mastered once you have learned the basic principles of spinning by working with the spindle. Although types of spindles vary widely, the method is basically the same for all of them. The most popular spindle used today is the one with the disc-shaped weight near the bottom of the shaft, and that is the type that is discussed in this chapter.

For centuries the spindle was the only tool used to spin yarn or thread. You may have read of Helen of Troy's famous golden spindle upon which she spun soft, dyed fleece, or the Egyptians' use of spindles to produce exceedingly fine threads for weaving. Ancient spindles varied greatly in size and shape, and so do spindles today. Small, delicate spindles are used for spinning fine, thread-like yarns. The shafts are often made of balsa, bamboo, or some other lightweight material. The weights, or whorls, may be anything from coins to discs made of clay or wood. Larger spindles are used for spinning medium to heavy yarns. These too are often made of wood, but most any suitable material may be used, so long as the spindle is not too light or too heavy for the yarn being spun on it.

While spindles can be purchased through some craft shops and spinning supply houses, such as those listed at the end of this book, you can also make your own. Children often come up with some very good ones—a dowel with a block of wood or a doorknob attached; a round, smooth, potato on a stick; a flattened ball of hardened clay on a stick; even a king-sized jar lid on a Tinker Toy stick. They all work!

A medium-sized, medium-weight spindle is the best choice for the beginner. Use a ⅜″ wooden dowel approximately 12″ to 14″ long for the shaft. In the beginning your yarn will probably be lumpy and on the thick side, but with practice you'll soon be spinning thin, uniform strands. When you reach this point, you may want to make yourself a light-weight spindle so that you can try spinning very fine yarns. The shaft for a light-weight spindle can be anything from a length of bamboo (old bamboo shades are great

for this) to a piece of thin doweling approximately 5″ or 6″ long.

The whorl should be uniform in shape so that the spindle will not wobble as it spins around. For the medium-sized spindle, the whorl could be a flat or bowl-shaped disc of clay or wood. Make the whorl 3″ to 4″ in diameter and ⅜″ to ¾″ thick. Make a hole the size of the spindle shaft right in the center of the whorl.

Some of the currently available craft clays are very satisfactory for making whorls. They can be kneaded and molded to make discs and flattened balls, and some types can even be rolled out like cookie dough so that many whorls can be made at one time. You can also make your own dough from materials in your kitchen. Here is a recipe that I found useful during my days as a grade-school teacher; it is for making whorls for tiny spindles, designed for spinning lightweight yarns. These home-made whorls are best used by more experienced spinners.

> ½ cup salt
> 1 cup water
> 1 cup flour
> 2 tsp. cream of tartar
> 1 tblsp. cooking oil
> A few drops food coloring (optional)

Mix ingredients well and cook over medium heat, stirring until the dough clings together, forming a ball. Turn out on a board. When cool enough to handle, knead several minutes. Roll out with a rolling pin (makes about 16 ⅜″-thick whorls). Use the rims of glasses, or cookie cutters, to cut out the weights. You can also lightly press designs into the clay with toothpicks, your fingers, or whatever catches your fancy. Be careful to keep the discs fairly thin (not over ⅜″) to avoid the formation of cracks while drying. Keep the whorls as uniform in shape as possible so that they will spin properly. Make a hole in the center of each weight to fit the size of the stick you are using for the spindle shaft. A 7″-long piece of ¼″ or ⅛″ doweling makes a good shaft, and a whorl with a diameter of from 1″ to 2″ is best.

After the whorls are shaped, you can either let them air-dry for a few days, or you can speed up the drying time by baking them first for several hours, with the oven set on warm. Then let them finish drying at room temperature, turning them

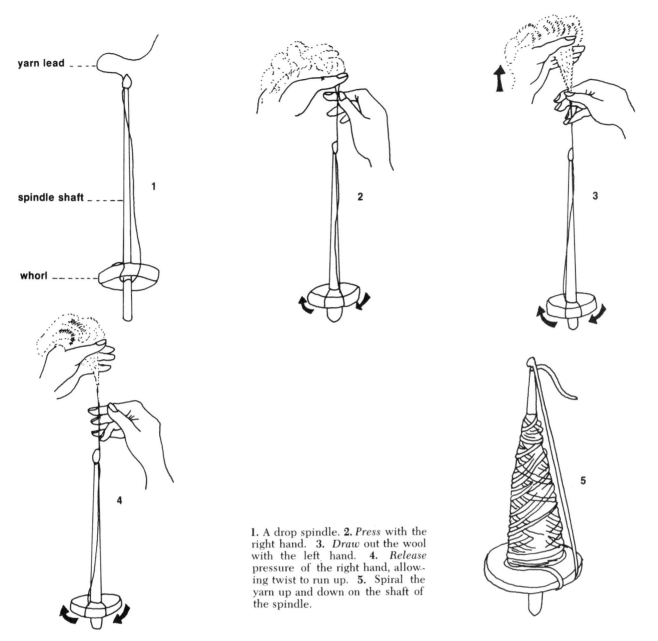

1. A drop spindle. 2. *Press* with the right hand. 3. *Draw* out the wool with the left hand. 4. *Release* pressure of the right hand, allowing twist to run up. 5. Spiral the yarn up and down on the shaft of the spindle.

occasionally, and checking to see that the hole in the center is the right size for the spindle shaft. If the hole is a little too small, enlarge it gently. If it is a little too large, don't be too concerned; you can always remedy the situation by gluing the whorl onto the shaft when it is dry.

When you have the whorl and the shaft ready, simply slip the whorl onto the spindle shaft, a few inches from the bottom, using a little white glue, if necessary, to insure a snug fit. Let the glue dry thoroughly. Then carve a little notch or groove at the top of the shaft—at the end opposite to the weight—to keep the yarn from slipping off the top of the shaft as you spin.

The drop spindle is now ready. The wool you use should have a medium staple length of at least 2½" and not more than 4" long. The rolag should be made of either "grease wool" or else lightly oiled and should be about an inch thick.

ATTACHING THE LEAD, AND JOINING UP

Tie a length of previously spun yarn, about 20" long, just above the whorl. Draw it down over the whorl and wind it around the shaft two or three times. Then bring the yarn back up to form a half-hitch, or loop, around the top, so that the yarn is held securely. Now your yarn lead is in place, and your spindle is ready for spinning.

Stand facing a table that's about waist-high and rest the spindle base on the table top for a moment. With your fingers, gently open the ends of the yarn lead so that they will easily catch and hold the loose fiber you are going to spin. Now wrap some of the wool from the rolag around the opened end of the yarn lead so that the ends overlap by about 3". Let the rest of the rolag lie over the back of your left hand and arm so that it is out of the way. Rolags are easiest to handle when they are no more than 8″ to 10″ long.

Hold the joined pieces firmly between your left thumb and forefinger, and raise your left arm so that the spindle rests lightly on the top of the table. With your right hand, give the top of the spindle a quick, clockwise turn. As the twist begins to travel up the strand, gradually release your hold on the joining point. Move your left hand up a little so that the twist will join the two ends into one firm strand. Now you're ready to learn to spin.

SPINNING

Now that the rolag and lead are joined, and you are holding the wool in your left hand, again give the spindle a clockwise spin. After turning the spindle, move the right hand back up and press on the yarn, just below the left hand. Then with your left hand draw out 2″ or 3″ of wool from the rolag. When you have done so, release your hold on the yarn with the right hand so that the twist can run up into the drawn-out wool. You have just spun your first few inches of yarn. (Don't let the twist run up past the fingers of the left hand, though, or you'll have a tangled mess instead of a rolag.)

Basically, the job of the left hand is to draw out the wool from the rolag. The right hand turns the spindle, then moves back up to help regulate the twist by alternately pressing and releasing the strand.

Let's go through that again. As the spindle turns beneath your hands, press firmly on the yarn with your right hand. Draw out more wool with the left; then release the hold with the right hand so that the twist can run up. *Press—draw—release.* Practice these steps until you have the idea.

After you've spun a foot or so of yarn, take the spindle from the table top, so that it can twirl freely beneath your hands. The spindle will have more momentum when allowed to hang freely, and the weight of it will gently stretch your yarn. Don't let the spindle turn backward, or it will untwist the yarn.

With a little practice, you'll learn how often to give the spindle another clockwise turn. Many spinners turn it too often when they are learning, and their yarn becomes too tightly twisted. Others, concentrating on drawing out the fleece, forget to keep the spindle from stopping, and may even allow it to turn backward. When this happens, the yarn unwinds itself, becomes weak, and may break.

When your length of newly spun yarn becomes so long that the spindle nearly reaches your feet, let the base of the spindle rest on the floor for a second while you place the unspun rolag between your knees. This keeps it from unwinding, and frees both hands to wind your yarn onto the spindle shaft above the whorl. When you have wound yarn about halfway up the shaft, spiral it back downward toward the whorl. Keep winding in this manner so that a nice, smooth cone of yarn begins to form on the spindle shaft.

When winding the yarn on, leave enough for a new lead. Wind it a few times beneath the whorl, bring it up to form a new loop at the top, and you are ready to spin again.

While some kinkiness is desirable in newly spun yarn, it should not be too tightly twisted. If it is very kinky, you are probably not drawing out the fiber quickly enough. Or, you may be concentrating so hard on turning the spindle that you turn it *too* often, never allowing it to slow down sufficiently before giving it another spin. Relax! Before long you'll be drawing out the fiber quickly and smoothly, and at the same time, controlling the twist so that the yarn is soft, even and not overspun.

If your yarn breaks, and the spindle crashes to the table top or floor, the yarn is not twisted tightly enough. Put in more twist before drawing out any more of the fiber. Sometimes it helps to go back to the supported spindle method for a while; put the spindle in a bowl and twirl it. If there is no downward pull, the yarn can't break as easily. Once you learn to put enough twist in the wool, however, go back to the practice of letting the spindle hang unsupported unless you are spinning very delicate yarns.

As you draw out the fiber, don't hold your hands too close together, or you won't be able to pull the fiber out fast enough. On the other hand, if you hold your hands too far apart, you'll have thin, stringy spots in the yarn. It takes practice.

If the spindle seems to stop turning very quickly, try twirling the spindle harder, or else try to thin down the rolag so that you can spin a thinner yarn. It may also be that you need a heavier spindle.

When spinning shorter, finer fibers, you'll find that it's easier if you use a shorter draw, pulling out the fiber in shorter lengths. You may also have to twist the fibers more tightly, and work with a thicker rolag.

After the spindle has quite a cone of yarn wound on it, you'll want to remove it, and finish your yarn as described in chapter five. Save some of the yarn you've spun to put a new yarn lead on your spindle.

Some spinners enjoy working on spindles so much that they never buy a wheel. If you travel often, and want a relaxing pastime, a drop spindle may be just the thing for you. I've spent many days spinning on a spindle next to a campfire, my old enamel dyepot steaming away, the newly spun yarn simmering in a brilliant yellow bath of "marigold stew" or "sagebrush soup."

IV

Spinning on the Treadle Wheel

There are many types of spinning implements available today, from the traditional spindles and wheels to some modern versions such as electric spinners and attachments which increase speed and efficiency. There are even spinner heads which can be mounted on a treadle base—such as that of an old sewing machine—and used to spin thick, attractive yarns. With all of the variety, however, the most popular spinning devices are still the simple drop spindle discussed in the last chapter and the treadle, or flax, wheel discussed here.

A spinning wheel is basically a drop spindle placed horizontally that is able to revolve at a faster speed because it has a drive wheel. Once you have learned to spin on a drop spindle, therefore, you will find that learning to spin on a wheel is merely a matter of sufficient practice.

Before you start to spin, take some time to learn the various parts of the spinning wheel and what the function of each part is. One illustration shows a traditional treadle wheel with the parts labeled; the other shows an upright or parlor wheel, a version of the treadle wheel.

Before attempting to spin, remove your shoe and spend some time just treadling your wheel with your bare foot to get the feel of the wheel. First treadle rapidly, then gradually more slowly until the treadling action is regular and just barely fast enough to keep the wheel going around continuously. You should practice this until it becomes automatic. Practice stopping and restarting your wheel, using only your foot, until it becomes almost automatic.

When you are ready to start spinning for the first time, it's a good idea to have a friend nearby to help. You will be treadling and at the same time trying to concentrate on what your hands are doing. Your friend can help by making sure the wheel doesn't stop. After a short time, your hands and foot will become coordinated, and you will be able to spin quite easily on your own.

ATTACHING THE LEAD, AND JOINING UP

Tie a length of previously spun yarn onto the bobbin. Draw this lead yarn around one of the hooks (or "hecks") nearest you, then through the eye of the spindle, on the same side as the hook you are using. Pull the lead yarn through the orifice or opening at the end of the spindle, using a bent paper clip or a tiny crochet hook to help. Open the end of the lead, fanning it out as for spindle spinning, so that the wool can be caught by it and easily joined. Now wrap some loose, carded wool from the rolag around the opened end of the lead, overlapping it 2″ or 3″. Hold the ends firmly between your left thumb and forefinger.

With your right hand, turn the large wheel clockwise, and begin to treadle slowly and regularly. Now that there is a yarn lead attached, you'll feel a definite pull from the wheel against your hand. The treadling will feel different too. The twist will start to build up in the yarn between the orifice and your left hand. Gradually release your hold on the yarn, sliding the left hand back, away from the wheel. The twist will join the two overlapped ends into one strand of yarn.

SPINNING A WOOLEN YARN

Stop treadling for a moment, but keep your left hand in the same position. With your right hand, draw out a few more inches of wool from the rolag. Begin treadling again very slowly, removing the left hand so that the twist can run up into the wool, right up to the fingers of the right hand. (Be careful not to let the twist go beyond the drawing hand itself, and up into the rolag.) The pull from the wheel will help somewhat in drawing the wool.

Begin drawing out wool again, keeping the right hand behind the left. As the right hand draws the fiber out, the left stays near the orifice, regulating the twist. When you have spun a foot or two of yarn, allow the pull of the wheel to wind the yarn onto the bobbin. Then begin to spin again. With a little practice, you'll become quite skillful at drawing out the wool quickly and smoothly and just fast enough to keep ahead of the twist as it travels up the strand.

Most spinners I know prefer to use the right hand to draw the fiber, and the left to control the

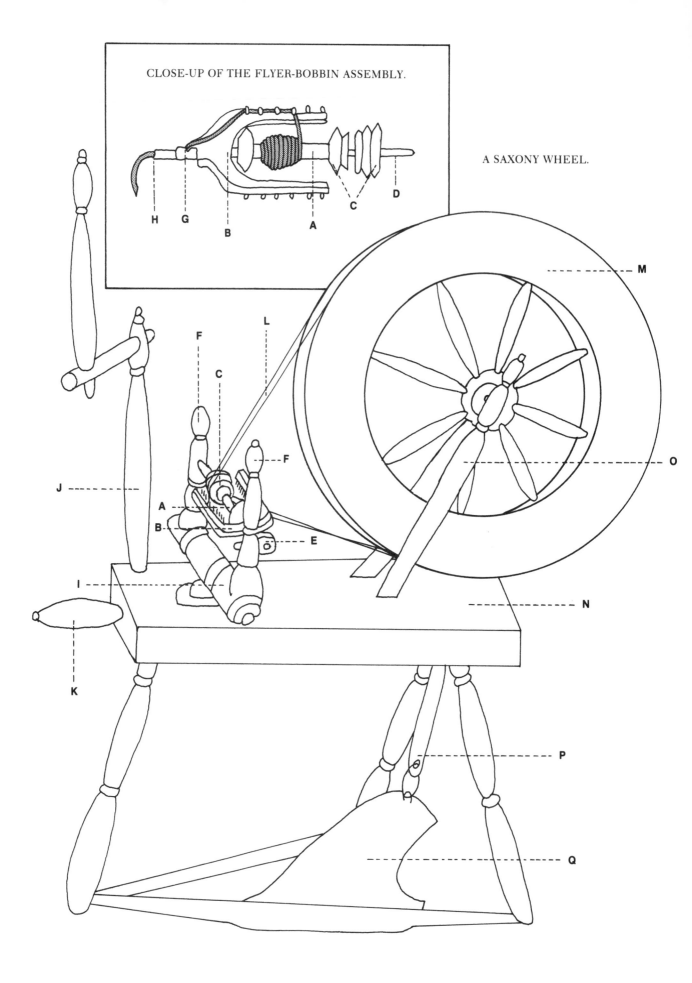

CLOSE-UP OF THE FLYER-BOBBIN ASSEMBLY.

A SAXONY WHEEL.

KEY TO THE FIGURES

A. *Bobbin.* The bobbin holds the spun yarn. It turns on the spindle shaft; the yarn is automatically wound onto the bobbin when the wheel is in operation.

B. *Flyer.* A horseshoe-shaped device, the flyer is turned by the flyer pulley. It has guide hooks, or "hecks," on each arm.

C. *Pulleys.* The two small wheels that are part of the spinning mechanism. One pulley is attached to the bobbin; the other turns the flyer.

D. *Spindle shaft.* The metal shaft that is attached to the flyer and that runs through the bobbin and pulleys.

E. *Bearings.* Two leather pieces, one on each maiden, that hold the spindle shaft in place.

F. *Maidens.* The upright pieces that support the flyer mechanism.

G. *Eye.* The hole between the foremost leather bearing and the flyer. The yarn goes onto the hooks of the flyer and through the eye.

H. *Orifice.* The opening at the end of the spindle shaft, through which the yarn is spun and wound onto the bobbin. Since the size of the orifice determines the thickness of the yarn that can be spun, the larger the orifice, the better.

I. *Mother-of-all.* The wooden bar that holds the maidens.

J. *Distaff.* The distaff can be used to hold certain types of unspun fiber (such as flax) for spinning. It is not used in spinning wool.

K. *Tension screw.* The tension screw adjusts the amount of tension on the driving band so that the rate of winding and the amount of twist in the yarn are controlled.

L. *Driving band.* The cord which runs between the pulleys and the large wheel.

M. *Drive wheel.* The large wheel.

N. *Bench.* The table upon which the spinning mechanism rests.

O. *Uprights.* The two arms that support the drive wheel.

P. *Footman* (also called pitman). A bar that connects the treadle to the axle of the drive wheel. Sometimes a cord is used instead of a wooden bar.

Q. *Treadle.* The part upon which the foot rests in order to operate the wheel. A bar and pins hold the treadle in place between the front legs (treadle bar).

AN UPRIGHT OR PARLOR WHEEL.

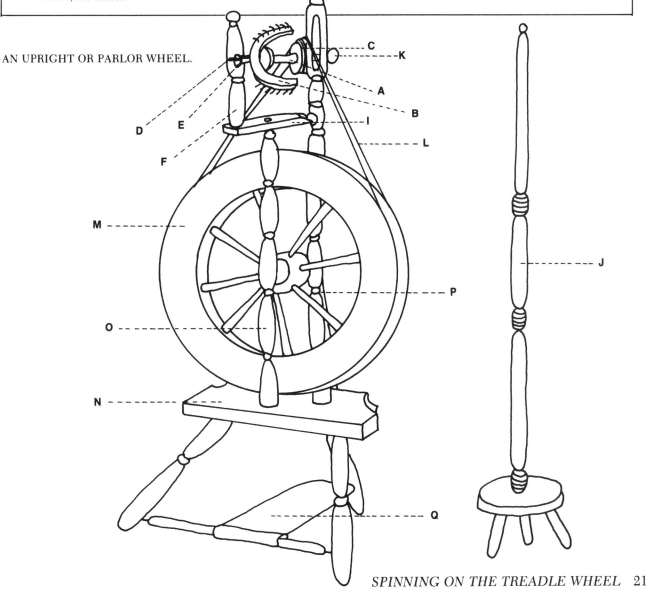

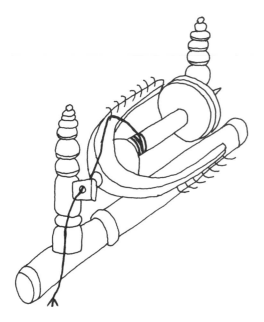

Attaching the yarn lead

The right hand draws the fiber as the left hand regulates the amount of twist.

twist. The left hand works between the right hand and the wheel.

After you've worked with wool, you may want to experiment with other fibers. When spinning longer fibers (6″ or more in length) you can draw out longer lengths of the fiber at a time. Shorter, finer, or slightly slippery ones will require a shorter draw. The length of the draw should be about the same as the length of the fiber. The amount of tension on the driving band makes a difference too. Usually, shorter fibers are more easily spun with less tension, and longer fibers spin better with increased tension.

As you spin, you'll have to move the yarn from one guide hook to another fairly often so that the bobbin fills evenly. You'll also have to increase the tension on the driving band as more yarn accumulates on the bobbin. When the bobbin is full, you can slip it off and replace it with another. You can also slip the driving band off one of the pulleys so that it is very slack, and then wind the yarn right off the bobbin without removing it. It's really best, however, to have several bobbins. New ones can be purchased in several sizes, according to bobbin length. You can also buy bobbin holders, some of which attach right to your wheel.

Many treadle wheels have two grooves in the flyer pulley. Each groove has a different diameter so that it's possible to spin either a tightly twisted worsted yarn using the deeper groove, or a loosely twisted and lofty woolen yarn using the shallower one.

SPINNING A WORSTED YARN

As you read in chapter two, there are actually two methods of spinning: the woolen method, which was described in the preceding section, and the worsted method. The principles are basically the same, but in the worsted method, which is usually reserved for very long fibers, the right hand is between the left one and the wheel. The right hand therefore moves between the wheel and the left hand, drawing the fibers fan-wise over the forefinger of the left hand, which is held stationary. The tension is set so that the fiber is drawn rather rapidly.

Locks of wool are also spun by the worsted method. The wool is held in the left hand, and the right hand draws out the fiber from the cut end of the lock. Most spinners feed the fibers into the twisting strand at a slight angle, allowing the fibers of the lock to slide smoothly over the forefinger of the left hand. The best locks for spinning "in the grease" are those in which the lanolin is still soft. The locks should be long and reasonably clean. They should also be sorted first so that straight ones are not mixed with very crimped ones. Traditionally, locks are spun with no teasing or combing, but sometimes I do tease the fibers apart a little—working from the cut end—so that they draw out with greater ease.

PROBLEMS BEGINNERS HAVE

1: The yarn is pulled through the hands too rapidly. Adjust the tension on the driving band so that it is a little more slack.

2: The yarn is very tightly twisted. Stop treadling, and unwind the yarn somewhat so that it has the right amount of twist. Then begin treadling again—only more slowly—and concentrate on drawing out the wool more quickly. Increasing the tension on the driving band may help too.

3: *The yarn breaks easily.* Allow more twist to run into the fiber before letting it wind onto the bobbin. Hold the yarn back until it is stronger and more tightly twisted. Experiment with the tension on the driving band, too—sometimes that makes a difference.

4: *The yarn doesn't wind onto the bobbin as fast as it should.* Check to see if the yarn is caught somewhere—on the orifice, or around the guide hooks, perhaps? Also be sure that both the spindle shaft and the inside of the bobbin are clean. Try changing the tension. As a last resort, put on a new driving band.

5: *The band repeatedly jumps out of the wheel grooves.* First tighten the tension a little. If that doesn't do the trick, check the alignment of the wheel and pulleys. You can remedy this by adjusting the uprights. The maidens which hold the leather bearings can also be adjusted somewhat so that the spinning mechanism can be moved slightly to one side or the other.

6: *Lumpy yarn.* Most new spinners have lumpy yarn, but practice and careful carding eliminates much of this. You can try to work the lumps out as you spin, but it's time-consuming.

7: *The wool in the rolag bunches up so that it's hard to draw the fiber out.* Beginners often grasp the rolag too tightly, bunching up the wool in a mass. Let it rest lightly in your hand.

8: *The yarn flies off the hooks as you spin.* Nothing serious here; just slow down a little.

9: *It takes so much time to stop and pick up another rolag every little while.* For more continuous spinning, place several rolags on your lap at one time so that a new one can be attached very smoothly and quickly, and with no interruption. If you are spinning fiber in roving form, place several of the lengths of rove horizontally across your lap. Overlap the ends so that they are very easy to join.

V
Finishing the Yarn

After you have spun your yarn, some finishing touches will be necessary before the yarn is ready for use.

Newly spun yarn should be removed from the bobbin and temporarily stored until it is to be finished. If I plan to ply my yarn—that is to spin several strands together—I usually wind it onto the spools of a "Lazy Kate," which is actually just a type of spool rack. Sometimes yarn that is to be plied can also be loosely wound into balls for short-term storage. I always wash my yarn after plying it.

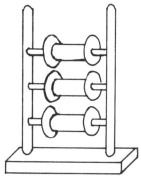

An upright "Lazy Kate." Some types have more than three bobbins.

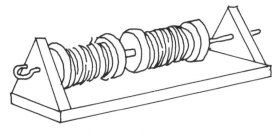

A two-bobbin, side-by-side "Lazy Kate." This type can be placed upon the lap while plying.

If I plan to use the yarn "as is," it must be washed first, so I skein it on some type of yarn winder. I've seen spinners toss a ball of newly spun or plied yarn into a pail of soapy water to wash it, but when this is done, it's difficult to be certain that the yarn on the inside of the ball is really clean. Yarn that is to be dyed must be especially clean and free of traces of spinning oil or grease. Skeins are much easier to handle, and the yarn dries rapidly after washing.

WINDING THE YARN

Yarn winders are fascinating. Many of the types used in the past are still available to spinners today in the form of reproductions. If you're fortunate, you may even come across an antique now and then.

Many old-fashioned yarn winders, though not all of them, measured the yarn in loops two yards in circumference. Forty turns of the winder made a "knot" of 80 yards, and the spinner tied a small knot in the yarn at that point. When seven "knots" had been wound, there were 560 yards of yarn, or one skein. Today the term "skein" is used more loosely, meaning any hank of yarn, but years ago, yarn was carefully measured.

Niddy-Noddies

One of the simplest and most popular yarn winders is the niddy-noddy. The origin of the name is the subject of much conjecture. I like to think that perhaps the granny (who was commonly called the "niddy" in many families) often sat and skeined the yarn, and that her head and the skeining device she used nodded in rhythmic enjoyment; hence the term "niddy-noddy."

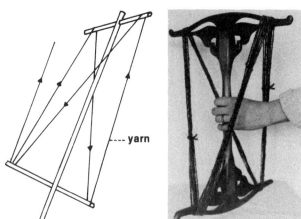

Niddy-noddies.

This winder consists of a center post and two crossarms, set at right angles to each other. All the limbs extending from the center post have a rim, except one. The end of the spun yarn is tied to this rimless piece, and the yarn is then wound on, as the niddy-noddy is rocked back and forth. The skein is then secured in several places with cord, the ends of the yarn tied together, and the skein slipped off by pulling it over the end without a rim.

Many of the craftsmen who make and restore wheels will also make niddy-noddies and other types of yarn winders. Some are copies of colonial pieces, others are not, and they can be purchased unfinished or stained. Some can even be taken apart, so that they are easy to transport.

Swifts

A swift, or "swiss," is a folding yarn winder which can be fastened to the edge of a table. The yarn is attached to one of the crossbars, and one hand guides the yarn into the V-shaped groove formed by the collapsible arms. The swift rotates freely and can also be used when winding skeins into balls of yarn. Most swifts are adjustable so that as many as a dozen different sizes of skeins can be wound.

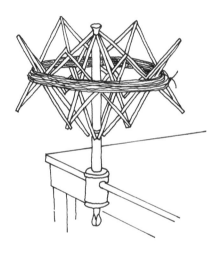

A swift.

Swifts can often be purchased in knit shops or through craft shops and supply houses selling to spinners and weavers. Most types can be used both vertically and horizontally and clamp to tables; a few models have floor stands as well.

Winding Reels

Winding reels, sometimes called winding blades, are not as common as other types of winders. Many of them resemble windmills. The arms (usually four of them) are mounted on the side of a supporting center post so that they turn freely. A piece of wood is attached at a right angle to the end of each arm. Three of these pieces of wood have double rims, but the fourth does not. As in the case of the niddy-noddy, the yarn can be removed easily from the rimless edge.

Occasionally one sees these reels, or reproductions of them, for sale, but they are rare. Perhaps you are fortunate enough to have an antique winding reel of your own.

Front

Side

Front and side views of a click reel.

Click Reels

The click reel, sometimes called the clock reel, is a special type of skeiner. Built in the same general shape as earlier winding reels, it often has a supporting base with legs. Usually there are four or six arms on the reel—sometimes more—and there is a mechanism which counts the revolutions. On most click reels, the arms measure approximately two yards, and after 40 turns the reel clicks loudly so that the person winding the yarn knows that 80 yards, or one knot, has been wound.

Click reels are lovely pieces; some are quite plain but others are beautifully turned and carved. Most have spools for yarn and racks to hold the spools. Some spinning and weaving supply houses stock click reels from time to time.

Making a Temporary Yarn Winder of Your Own

If you are planning to do a lot of spinning, you'll no doubt want to purchase or make one of the traditional types of yarn winders. You can, however, make a temporary winder out of a rustproof coat hanger. Grasp the hanger at the midpoint of the long, bottom section of wire, and pull downward until the hanger is diamond-shaped—four corners—with a hook at the top. Then bend the corners in a little so that yarn can be wound around them. Wind your yarn on the hanger, tie the skein with cotton cord in a few places, and knot the two loose ends of the yarn so that they can't unwind. Always use cotton cord; it does not shrink when you wash or dye the yarn and it will therefore not become tight and constrict the skein.

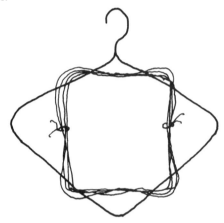

A yarn winder made from a rustproof coat hanger.

Your skein can then be slipped off the hanger and washed gently or soaked. This little yarn winder may not hold very large amounts of yarn, but it is especially handy because the wet skein can be slipped back onto the hanger again to dry. Then all you have to do is hang up the winder by the hook at the top. When the yarn is dry, the skein can be slipped off easily by pushing in on the corners of the flexible wire.

PLYING THE YARN

Plying simply means twisting several strands together. The decision on whether or not to ply your yarn is often based upon the use to which it will be put. Many weavers, for instance, prefer a carefully spun single-ply yarn even to use as a warp. Knitters, on the other hand, often prefer plied yarns which have a more "finished" look. There are really no hard-and-fast rules as far as plying is concerned. Basically it's a matter of personal preference. Yarns spun from short or slick fibers will be stronger and more durable after plying. Long, strong fibers, therefore, are usually not plied. Flax, for example, is seldom plied. When plying yarns of different fibers, be sure that they have about the same amount of elasticity and shrinkage.

Spinners often use the terms "S-twist" and "Z-twist," which refer to the direction of the twist in the yarn. When the spindle shaft or wheel is turned clockwise, a Z-twist is put into the yarn. When the spindle shaft or wheel is turned counterclockwise, the result is an S-twisted yarn. Usually, single strands of yarn are Z-twisted while two or more strands are usually plied with an S-twist. Each time you ply more yarns, you spin them in the direction *opposite* to that spun before. Two Z-twisted single yarns, therefore, would be plied with an S-twist. If you wanted to combine two S-twisted double-plies, you would spin them with a Z-twist again to form the four-ply yarn.

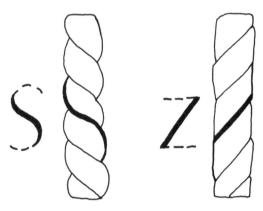

Left: S-twisted yarn. The wheel is turned counterclockwise. *Right:* Z-twisted yarn. The wheel is turned clockwise.

Plying on a Spindle

Start by attaching a yarn lead; if you are going to ply with an S-twist, attach an S-twisted yarn lead. Now tie two Z-twisted single strands to the lead, using any type of a knot. Place one strand on each side of the middle finger of your left hand.

For smooth, efficient plying, yarns should be wound so that they will unwind easily. Many spinners simply place jars or paper bags on the floor, and put a ball of single-ply yarn in each. That way, the balls can't roll around, and they stay clean. Other spinners with hand spindles mount cones of single-ply yarn upright on a stand of some sort. Still others prefer Lazy Kates, or similar bobbin holders, because the yarn rolls off the bobbins so easily.

When you are ready, give the spindle a counterclockwise spin with your right hand so that the twist is reversed this time. Allow the strands to pass easily and rapidly, putting in as much twist as you like, until the spindle nearly touches the floor. Then slip off the yarn leader and wind the plied yarn onto the spindle shaft. Plying is faster than spinning a single strand, and you'll find it quite simple. The important thing is to feed the yarns evenly so that the plied yarn is smooth and even.

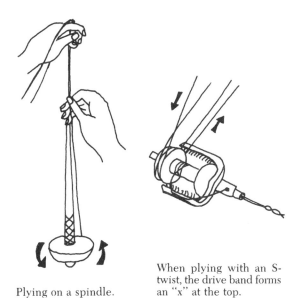

Plying on a spindle.

When plying with an S-twist, the drive band forms an "x" at the top.

Plying on a Wheel

Tie two Z-twisted yarns to an S-twisted yarn lead, as for spindle plying. Then pull the knot through the orifice and the eye of the spindle and around the first guide hook. Adjust the tension on the driving band so that it is fairly tight. Place the strands on either side of the middle finger of the left hand. With the right hand, give the wheel a counter-clockwise turn so that the direction of twist is reversed. The driving band will form an "X" at the top. Treadle quickly and regularly. Sing a song if that helps you keep the rhythm. Concentrate on allowing the yarns to pass freely and smoothly. Don't hold back on one strand more than another. Any unevenness in feeding the yarns, or in treadling, will produce a yarn that is unevenly plied. After you have become proficient at plying you can experiment a bit by deliberately plying the yarns unevenly to create some interesting effects. But save this until such time as you can produce an evenly plied yarn.

Some spinners ply very loosely so that the yarns are soft and fluffy. Others prefer the appearance of a firmer, more tightly plied yarn. It will depend to some extent on whether the yarn is woolen or worsted and on how the yarn will be used.

WASHING THE YARN

When you remove the yarn from the wheel, spindle, or yarn winder, it will be a mass of loose kinks and twists—certainly not the most manageable yarn you've ever seen. To make the yarn smooth and to set the twist, you will need to rewash it.

Begin by soaking the skeins in one or two lukewarm soap-and-water baths. Then put the yarn in a lukewarm rinse bath. If necessary, use several rinse baths. This will remove the lanolin or spinning oil so that later on if you want to dye the yarn it will be grease-free. If, however, you have spun wool fleece "in-the-grease," and you want to leave some natural lanolin in the yarn, steep the skeins in cool, clear water—no soap or detergent—until they are clean. If the yarn is quite soiled, it may be necessary to use a very little soap.

After rinsing, blot the wet yarn gently in a towel. If you have used a coat hanger to skein your yarn, simply slip the skein back on the hanger and hang by its hook. The yarn should be under some tension as it dries. If you made your skeins on a regular yarn winder, hang them on a line to dry. Attach weights to the lower ends of the skeins so that there is enough tension on the yarn to straighten it as it dries. Clean rocks, bricks, and boards (not *too* heavy, though!) make good weights. Remember to dry the skeins in the shade.

Folding a skein of yarn: Twist the skein . . . then slip one end through the other.

When the yarn is dry it will be free of kinks and oiliness. The twist will be set so that it will no longer unwind. The skeins can then be folded for storage, if you wish. To fold a skein, simply twist it—holding one hand on each end—and slip one end loop through the other.

Yarns from animal fibers other than wool can be treated in much the same way as woolen yarns except that they seldom need to soak as long. Use a dog shampoo if the fiber is quite dirty.

Yarns made from vegetable fibers often need no washing, or else very little, since they are usually purchased in a clean state. Because many of them are spun damp or wet, they tend to be smooth yarns, and often don't even need to be immersed in water to set the twist. If, for some reason, they are twisted so tightly that they need to be rewet and weighted, use clear, warm water.

STORAGE OF HOMESPUN YARN

If your homespun yarns, or articles made of them, are likely to attract moths, store them if possible in a cedar chest. Otherwise, use mothballs, or store them in bags with small pieces of cedar. They will remain lovely for many years.

VI

Obtaining a Spinning Wheel

It's a good idea to actually know something about spinning before you decide to buy a wheel. If you have read the preceding chapters, you should have a basic understanding of how a wheel operates, and you should be familiar enough with the craft of spinning to be able to try any wheel before buying it.

It's difficult to say whether you should buy an old wheel or a new one; so many types are available today. In addition to lovely old antiques there are some very good reproductions as well as some fine wheels that are modern in design.

An old wheel, especially if it is a family heirloom, naturally is of great sentimental value to its owner, and it may have some value simply because it is an antique. It's great fun to spin on an old wheel, such as this, *if it is in good condition.* On the other hand, an old wheel that is warped, wobbly, and out of balance is an abomination to use. Unless you can find an old wheel that is in reasonably good condition or one that can be restored without too much expense, you should consider purchasing a new wheel.

HOW TO SHOP FOR AN OLD WHEEL

Finding a good antique wheel is often more than a matter of luck. A little knowledge and preparation can increase your chances of finding just the wheel you want. Become familiar with the various types of wheels, and learn the parts so that you can tell whether any are missing. Remember that the great wheel is the large one that is usually turned by hand. It is impressive and beautiful, but the small treadle, or flax, wheel is the more efficient of the two. Both hands are freed for spinning, and you can spin just about any fiber on the treadle wheel.

When you shop for your wheel, carry along with you a length of cotton cord (such as parcel post string), a scissors, and—if you wish to try spinning—a length of yarn to use as a leader, and, if you already know how to spin, a little carded wool.

Quite often the driving band on the wheel is missing, or the person selling the wheel has put on a new one that is wrong for the wheel. Sometimes one sees wheels sporting slippery nylon driving bands, or leather or yarn ones which are too stretchy to do any good, or even driving bands that are much too large for the grooves on the wheels. (I once saw a heavy clothesline used as a driving band.) Don't be afraid to ask if you can attach a new driving band, if it needs one, so that you can pedal the wheel. Use your cotton cord for this.

Examine the wheel carefully for missing parts. The large drive wheel should turn smoothly and easily. The small pulleys should also turn freely, although if they don't, the solution may be as simple as removing greasy lanolin buildup from the metal spindle shaft and the inside of the bobbin. You should be able to very carefully remove the small pulleys and the flyer from the metal shaft by turning one or both of the maidens, or upright posts, that support the spinning mechanism.

Beware of warped, wobbly, or badly worn parts. These will probably have to be replaced. You needn't worry too much about minor squeaks or groans. Most of these can be remedied by oiling. Rattling or grating sounds might indicate a problem, however, and these should be investigated. Most old wheels were held together by wooden pegs. Nails anywhere indicate a "repair job" of some sort. Old wheels were usually made so that they could be taken apart. If the legs are glued in, for example, the wheel probably has been tampered with. I've even seen cases where the two pulleys were glued or nailed together so that they could not turn separately as they should. If you plan to buy the wheel and have it repaired, keep a list or make a mental note of anything you feel a wheel repairman should be told.

If the distaff for flax spinning is missing, as it commonly is, don't worry. New distaffs that will fit most wheels are available if you want one. Because water is used to keep the fingers moist while spinning flax, some old wheels have a hole in the bench for a water dish.

If the footman is missing, tie a piece of cord or string between the treadle and the axle crank so that you can pedal the wheel. A footman is easy to replace or repair; so is a treadle, a leg, a maiden, a spoke or two in the wheel, or a leather bearing. Replacement of the mother-of-all, the tension screw, or the large drive wheel may be a little more expensive and time-consuming. Often the spindle shaft, the flyer, or one of the pulleys needs to be repaired or replaced, but this is not a major problem. Older flyer pulleys may have a left-handed thread. The pulleys should line up with the groove in the drive wheel. One spinner I know pounds in little wooden wedges at the bases of the uprights to remedy this.

If you find a wheel that's basically sound, but needs some repairs, try to locate a reputable wheel repairman and tell him the nature of the difficulty—before you buy the wheel, if possible. Most spinners know a wheel repairman who will understand what you are talking about when you tell him which parts of the wheel are missing or malfunctioning. If you don't know any spinners in your area, the proprietors of craft shops or members of weaving guilds may be able to help you to locate a spinner or a good wheel repairman. It pays to contact someone who knows old spinning wheels because each wheel is unique, and replacement and repair must be right for your particular wheel. The wheel repairman can also tell you about how much it will cost for necessary repairs and whether or not the wheel is worth the repairs. Many times the cost is small. If the person selling the wheel knows that the wheel is less than perfect and that you will have to have work done on it, he may sell the wheel at a very reasonable price.

Just how much an old wheel will cost is a hard question to answer; so much depends upon the age and condition of the wheel in question. If you have ever shopped for antiques, you know that prices vary as do dealers' reputations. Don't be in a hurry; shop carefully. There are still many lovely old wheels around. You'll find wheel hunting a real adventure, and you may end up with exactly what you want.

Reconditioning an Old Wheel

Even if major repairs are unnecessary, most antique wheels will need some attention. Start by examining the driving band. Most treadle wheels have a single, continuous band connecting the drive wheel and the two small pulley wheels that are part of the spinning assembly. The two loops or halves of this continuous band cross on the underside. Some treadle wheels have only one pulley and only one band running between it and the drive wheel. There are even some wheels with two separate driving bands, one to each pulley; the majority, however, have the one long driving band, drawn twice around, as described above.

If the driving band needs replacing, attach a new one of cotton cord. As I indicated before, I prefer parcel post string. Use a size that fits the grooves of the wheel. Some spinners also use Venetian blind cord, or even candle wicking. Don't use anything that will slip or stretch— leather, for example—or you will be constantly taking up the slack and adjusting the tension on the band as you spin. To replace the band, turn the tension adjustment so that the mother-of-all is situated about half as far as it can be moved toward the large wheel. Then draw the band around twice, in two loops, crossing the two loops between the wheel and the pulleys on the underside. When you have the band in place, tie a small knot, or sew or splice the ends together. Then apply a bit of white glue to the joined ends to make the joining more secure. When the glue has dried, put on a dab of beeswax at the joining point. Then turn the tension screw to take up any slack in the driving band.

Check the axle to be certain that it is clean. Remove the pulleys with the flyer and the bobbin, to be sure that the spindle shaft is free of greasy lanolin and rust. A light sanding and a little grease solvent will clean a rusty or sticky spindle in no time. It's also a good idea to put on a light coat of metal polish, if you have some handy. The insides of the bobbin and flyer pulleys should be cleaned out by pushing a pipe cleaner through several times. It may also be necessary to smooth a few rough spots on the flyer hooks, or "hecks," which might otherwise snag the yarn or keep it from passing easily onto the bobbin.

Lubricate the axle that supports the large wheel with petroleum jelly or graphite (such as lead pencil shavings). Grease the tension screw, too. Oil all other movable parts with 3-in-1 Oil, regular household oil, or sewing machine oil. Don't forget such things as leather bearings, the area at the top of the footman, the spinning mechanism, and any movable parts on the treadle support.

If the wheel has been refinished, check the groove that the driving band rests in to be certain that it has not been refinished too. If by chance it has, roughen it a bit so it won't be slippery. Apply some "Liquid Gold" or another wood conditioner to the finish on your wheel now and then. If your wheel has not been refinished, but simply rubbed with a good oil such as linseed or tung oil, don't forget to rub on a new coat occasionally to keep your wheel glowing.

HOW TO BUY A NEW WHEEL

Today's wheels come in all shapes and sizes, many with improvements for making spinning easier. You can purchase reproductions of old wheels, or ones that are quite modern in design. Most spinning and weaving shops, and spinning supply houses carry several types, from models costing less than a hundred dollars to more expensive ones. Again, your choice will depend upon your needs and tastes. If you plan to use the wheel a great deal, it's wise to pay a little more and get one that will hold up well through many years of hard use.

If possible, select a wheel made of hardwood. It will be heavier and more durable. Most good wheels are made of oak, cherry, black walnut, or a combination of these.

Most wheelmakers are very skilled in their craft, and will take the time to make you exactly what you ask for—even a careful copy of a particular wheel. They will put the parts together with pegs, as wheelmakers did years ago, and will make fancy, beautifully turned posts and legs for your wheel, using any wood you desire. Some even know how to spin, and can give you a demonstration so that you can be certain your wheel really works before you even take it home. Often wheelmakers add their own special little touches, such as rustproof spindles and hooks, or a specially made bobbin holder to fit your wheel.

As when shopping for an antique, know the parts of a wheel. Occasionally you'll find a less-than-honest fellow, out to make "a fast buck." My husband Wayne and I once spent a few eye-opening hours in a "Junque Shoppe" in northern Wisconsin. The proprietor, a tall and prepossessing fellow with a broad grin, told us to look around while he went into the work area adjoining the shop.

We began inspecting old dolls, glassware, and pieces of furniture, but my curiosity soon got the better of me because I heard such interesting noises coming from the workshop area. I walked through the door, and—wonder of wonders—the man was busily working on a spinning wheel.

It was a Saxony wheel, made of oak, rather small as wheels go. I asked him what the price would be, trying to sound as disinterested as possible. (Very difficult! My heart beats in double-time at the sight of a spinning wheel.)

"I'd like to get ninety-five dollars for it," he said, flipping his sandy hair out of his eyes. "And you can bet that's a bargain," he added, with a broad grin that displayed a double row of gigantic white teeth.

"Are you nearly finished with it?" (Again, trying to sound only mildly interested.)

"Sure, except for some sanding."

That was a reasonable price for a wheel at that time, but it seemed crudely made. There were only four very large bent hooks on each arm of the flyer. There should have been more. Then to my astonishment I discovered that there was no opening for the newly spun yarn to go through, no way for it to get to those four hooks or onto the bobbin! There was no means of adjusting the tension on the driving band either. Amazing!

By this time, Wayne had walked in. He eyed the wheel appraisingly. "How does it work?" he asked innocently enough.

"Well, I really don't have time to explain. The yarn goes around between this big wheel and the little ones. (He meant the driving band, and that's *not* where the yarn goes.) It'll spin good."

It would "spin good" all right, but it wouldn't spin yarn! We left, but not until we had told him what was wrong with the wheel. One could always set a planter filled with ivy on it, I suppose. Buy from someone who knows what he is doing.

MAKING YOUR OWN SPINNING WHEEL

There are many types of spinning wheel plans—everything from the type that uses scrap wood and bicycle parts to rather elaborate and detailed reproductions of old-fashioned wheels. The type you choose will depend upon your own personal needs and skills.

Sources for spinning wheel plans are listed in the "Sources of Supply" at the end of this book. Some of these wheels are beautiful as well as practical, and would make lovely family pieces to pass on to your heirs. I should mention, however, that some of the plans require a fair amount of know-how, especially where woods are concerned. Follow the plans carefully, or you may wish you'd simply bought a wheel in the first place.

VII

Spinning Other Animal Fibers

Once you have learned to spin wool, you may want to try spinning other animal fibers. The wide range of hair and fur fibers available to spinners makes it possible to create some unique and exciting yarns. Angora, alpaca, camel, and pet hair are just a few of the interesting fibers sold by shops and spinning and weaving supply houses at reasonable prices. The possibilities are endless. Long types, whether silky or coarse, are very strong and perfect for worsted yarns. Medium-length fibers are fine for woolen yarns; very short types—under an inch in length—can be carded with wool, flax, or another support fiber to add texture and color, and to create blends with a variety of uses.

Some shaggy animals have long, silky coats which can be clipped and spun. Others have combination coats—coarse guard hairs on the outside with soft, delicate undercoats. Both the outer coat and the undercoat can be spun in most cases, but the undercoat is most often sought by spinners because it is so soft and fine.

Hair and fur fibers are handled a bit differently from wooly ones. To prepare them for spinning, sort them first according to length, texture, waviness (if any), and color. Don't throw away the very short types. Use these for blends. Save the coarse types for a rough-textured yarn. After sorting, put the different types into separate containers and label them.

If you have purchased your hair or fur from a source that sells to spinners and weavers, the fibers will probably already be cleaned—and possibly sorted—for you. If, however, you have a friend who runs a children's petting zoo, or if you raise your own animals, you may have to settle for fiber that is dirty and possibly rather "fragrant" too. I have friends who regularly give me combings or "shed" fiber from a wide variety of animals, and much of it requires washing before spinning. The fiber often appears quite different after it is clean. Beneath that dusty or dirty coating might be a beautiful, incredibly soft fiber. Simply follow the special instructions on "Washing" and "Adding Oil" in chapter two.

Cotton carders are excellent for carding light, delicate types of fur. I use them for dog, cat, fox, rabbit, or similar undercoatings.

DOG AND CAT COMBINGS

Have you ever seen a furry collie cap, or a pair of mittens made from the combings of a Persian cat? The shaggy family dog or cat is a wonderful source of fiber for spinning. Some may try to tell you that pet combings, especially the shorter types, are just not worth the bother, but don't believe it. These fibers can add both color and texture to wool yarns, and also can be spun "as is," unless they are extremely short. After you've tried spinning these fibers, you may well find that the yarns you treasure most are the ones that come from your own pets.

Long, silky types are strong, lustrous, and easy to spin. The textural properties of long, coarse types make them worth trying also. Those with a medium staple length, 1″ to 4″ long, often are as soft as angora or mohair, and can be spun into soft, very fuzzy yarns. Very short combings, especially those that are soft and fine, can be carded with wool to obtain some exciting, colorful blends.

A few types of dog hair—such as poodle—are wavy or even quite curly. It depends somewhat upon the individual poodle; some have curlier coats than others, and some feel more "wooly." While people usually clip their poodles, rather than comb them for fiber, many poodles enjoy a good brushing, and will "shed" more hair during grooming than one might expect.

Although clippings can be used for spinning, combings are preferred. Combings provide the long, natural fiber ends to work with, and they do tend to be softer. The yarn from clippings will be coarser because of the presence of more guard hair from the outer coat.

Most pet combings will need some minor sorting. I begin with a minimal sorting for length and texture, usually just picking out the very short combings, or those which are especially coarse. If there are still any variations in fiber length after this initial sorting, I try to arrange the combings on the carders so that the long and short fibers are evenly mixed. That way, my yarn will have an even texture throughout, with no noticeable weak spots or irregularities. Colors can be separated or blended, as you prefer.

When spinning pet hair or fur that is short and

fine, remember to use a shorter draw; experiment a little until you have just the right amount of twist. If you don't twist the yarn tightly enough, it will break easily. It's also helpful to loosen slightly the tension on the driving band. These fine, downy types are a little more difficult to spin at first, but the lovely results make it worthwhile. If you feel that these fine hairs are too fluffy and fuzzy for some of your projects, or if you think they will shed too much, card them with some wool instead of using the pure fiber. Most newly spun yarns containing fur or hair will shed for awhile, but in time they shed less and less.

The many different types of dog and cat hair that can be used for spinning are quite surprising. I've probably spun over 50 types of dog combings. It's impossible to name my favorites, because there are so many types. Samoyed, collie, Newfoundland, and a great many others will give you a soft yarn that resembles angora. Poodle yarn and similar types will be very much like wool. Afghan hound combings can be spun into exceedingly soft, silky yarns. You can also spin wonderful yarns from the coats of mixed breeds, such as collie-shepherd, peke-a-poo, and cock-a-poo.

Combings from Persian, Angora, and other varieties of long-haired cats can be spun into very soft yarns—some of them quite silky. One of my favorites is a blend of cat combings and wool. Adding wool makes the cat combings go further and gives strength to the yarn. Occasionally, I card some "alley cat" with wool, too.

Lynx, fox, or wolf fiber can sometimes be purchased through spinning supply houses. If you are fortunate, you may know someone who raises some of these usually "wild" animals; I receive wolf and fox combings from friends who hand-raise them.

GOAT HAIR

Mohair

Mohair is the yarn made from the silky hair of the Angora goat. It is white, soft, and lustrous. The Angora goat is named for the old Turkish province of Angora, now called Ankara, and this animal was one of the first to be domesticated by man. Today, Angoras are raised in several parts of the world. Large numbers are found in the southern and western United States, especially in Texas.

Angoras have small heads, with curious floppy ears, large bodies, and sturdy, short legs. Adults sometimes weigh as much as 140 or 145 pounds, and the male has long, spiraling horns. The fleece often grows to a length of 11" or 12" or more, in a year's time, and it is clipped either once or twice annually.

Mohair is classified according to its waviness. Some locks are very tightly curled, others are not. Generally, there is little variation in the waviness on any one Angora goat—certainly not as much variation as on sheep. Mohair can be obtained in roving form, but the lock or fleece type is usually a little nicer to spin, especially if you obtain it from a young Angora. The locks should be open, not matted, and clean. Some spinning supply houses label the fleece as "fluffy fleece," "tight lock," or "flat lock," depending upon the tightness or waviness of the mohair. All three are satisfactory for spinning.

If the mohair is quite dirty, wash it as you would any other type of fur or hair. Handle it as little as possible when it's wet because it does have a tendency to tangle. Before teasing, carding or combing, add a little spinning oil-water mixture so that the fiber is easier to handle. With a good grade of mohair, carding may not even be necessary, and just a gentle teasing will do. If bits of straw or other unwanted matter remain, a thorough teasing or carding will remove much of the refuse.

Mohair can be spun by either the woolen or worsted method depending upon the length of the locks. More twist is needed than for wool. A blend of short mohair fleece and wool will give you a yarn that is both "wooly" and lustrous.

Cashmere

Cashmere is soft and silky, but often difficult to obtain. It comes from the Cashmere (or Kashmir) goat, native to Asia. It is usually associated with that area of the Himalayas referred to as Kashmir, and at one time this part of the world was known for its incredibly beautiful Kashmir shawls.

The Cashmere goat has a combination coat. On the outside the long, protective covering of hair, and underneath a soft down that varies from shades of creamy white to gray, brown, and black. Generally, the colder the climate, the heavier the coat, but even on a full-grown animal the amount of down is seldom more than four or five ounces. The fiber is obtained by combing rather than clipping, and it varies from 1½" to 3" in length.

After the animals are groomed, the fiber is sorted carefully because some of the coarse, outer hair must be removed from the down. This is time-consuming work, and probably explains why pure cashmere is so expensive. Sometimes you can purchase less expensive lots of cashmere and remove the outer hair yourself, or you can spin the hair-down mix into a coarse but interesting yarn.

Cashmere seldom needs washing, and often just a gentle teasing with the fingers will be sufficient to clean it. The only time I card cashmere is when I am blending it with another fiber.

I also like to add a little oil to facilitate spinning.

When spinning cashmere down, put in a little more twist than you would when spinning wool, and keep the tension on the driving band a little more slack.

Other Types of Goat Hair

Fiber from the short-haired varieties of goats that many people raise can be blended with other fibers to create yarns with different textures and different colors. The fibers are too short and slick, however, to spin without a support fiber.

Drawn goat hair of various types can also be purchased in bundles of long strands. This can be dampened slightly and spun into a coarse yarn, or else laid, unspun, into pieces of weaving.

CAMEL HAIR AND DOWN

When the word "camel" is mentioned, people usually think of either the one-humped Arabian (dromedary) or the two-humped Bactrian camel. Actually there are a number of other members of the camelidae family, and their hair and down can be used for spinning also.

Bactrian and Arabian Camels

The Bactrian camel, with its longer outer hair and very soft undercoat, is said to produce some of the finest down for spinning. The hair of the dromedary is also used to some degree.

When camels shed their heavy coats, the hair and down come out in large clumps. These clumps are saved and later sorted or combed to separate the long, coarse hair from the down. The coarse hair of the camel can be spun and used as a novelty yarn or cordage. It is also used to make rugs, brushes, and other things. The down, usually with a staple length of 1″ to 3″, can be spun alone or blended with other fibers. It does not mat, or felt, easily.

Camel down, or hair mixed with down, as well as the dark brown outer hair can be purchased from some spinning supply centers. If you do buy the hair-down mixture, you'll find that it isn't difficult to sort out the hair, and the lovely yarn spun from the down makes it worth the effort.

To prepare camel fiber for spinning, pull the coarse hair out as you gently take the clumps apart. Then tease the down with your fingers. The outer hair can be saved for worsted spinning, and the down used for woolen yarns. Both the hair and the down are easier to spin if oil, or oil-and-water emulsion, is added prior to carding or combing. Spin the down just as you would cashmere or a similar fiber. Put in more twist, and lessen the tension on the driving band.

Alpaca

The alpaca is one of four South American members of the camel clan, the others being the guanaco, the vicuna, and the llama. Both the llama and alpaca were developed from the wild guanaco; therefore the alpaca resembles the llama although it is smaller and has longer hair. Its curious, padded camel-feet and its heavy coat enable it to endure the rigors of life in the Andean highlands.

The alpaca is clipped once every year or once every two years. The fleece often grows to more than 20″ in length. The silky fiber ranges from white, tan, and gray, to red, dark brown, and black. Alpaca does not mat easily, and it is often blended with other fibers.

Alpaca can be obtained in both fleece and roving form. It is easy to card or comb, although those procedures are often not necessary. The addition of oil makes it even easier to spin. Alpaca is one of my favorites, and it can be spun into some truly exquisite yarns. It is strong, and needs little twisting.

Vicuna

The vicuna is the smallest and wildest of the South American camels. It has soft, silky wool that varies from red to brown. It is considered by some to be the ultimate in softness and fineness. At one time, these gentle and graceful creatures were hunted to near extinction, but fortunately today they are protected by law. Some attempts are even being made to domesticate them.

Centuries ago, the Inca Indians regularly caught and sheared vicunas, then released them to grow more wool. Only persons of royal blood were allowed to wear garments made of vicuna. Today, the people of the high Andes have great respect for these animals. Perhaps vicuna wool will become more readily available as man finds a way to raise the animals in greater numbers.

Llama

While the llama is primarily considered a beast of burden, its coat is also valuable. Although not quite as fine as alpaca, llama hair is still very satisfactory for spinning. It varies in color from white or cream to gray, brown, or black.

I have obtained llama combings from a friend who raises them, and also from an accomodating caretaker at a petting zoo. (While my son visited with the animals, I brushed a curious but cooperative llama.) The wool was not difficult to clean, and I added some oil before carding it. It was very easy to spin.

DEER AND ANTELOPE HAIR

Hairs from members of the deer and antelope families (moose, white-tailed and black-tailed deer, reindeer, and others) are, as a rule, short and slick. They can still be used for spinning if blended with a support fiber. Besides extending the support fiber, these hairs will supply texture and color.

People who raise tame deer are often willing to provide you with a sample for spinning if you offer to give them some of the yarn.

COW AND HORSE HAIR

Short- or medium-length hair from various cows and horses raised on farms or ranches can be used for spinning. The hair tends to be a bit coarse, but it is colorful, and a horse hair—or cow hair—wool blend can be used for making mats, bags, saddle blankets, and other useful items. Both the combings of "winter underwear" and the longer hair from the mane and tail of a horse or pony can be spun. Add a little oil-and-water emulsion for easier spinning. Unspun mane and tail hair can also be laid in as weft in weaving projects.

American Bison, or Buffalo

Because of structural differences, the bison is not really a true member of the buffalo family, but the two names are often used interchangeably. The buffalo is one of several types of wild cattle with hair or undercoating suitable for spinning. A full-grown bull is a formidable creature, often weighing a ton or more. The shoulders, neck, and head are covered by a thick mane of long, dark brown hair. Under the guard coat of the buffalo, there is a lovely, soft brown fiber which is prized by spinners.

I obtain most of my buffalo fiber from a family that raises these animals. They save the clumps of hair for me when the coats rise in the spring. Buffalo are not the most predictable of creatures, so my friends gather most of the fiber by walking along fences and removing clumps that are caught there. The hair and undercoat must be separated by hand, and because the fiber is so dusty, I usually wash it gently before working with it further. Then I oil it. Carding removes the last bits of straw and other unwanted matter. I have spun the coarse, dark brown hair from the shoulders, but I much prefer the delicate undercoat.

Musk Ox

The musk ox is related to the ox and the sheep. It sheds a soft, grayish-brown undercoat, called qiviut, which is spun by Eskimos into exceedingly fine yarns. Qiviut is stronger, longer, and finer than cashmere, but at the present time, with a few exceptions, only Eskimos are allowed to possess it. This law was passed in order to generate a new industry for Eskimos, and they are now creating and selling beautiful scarves, shawls, sweaters, and other articles made from this delicate fiber. Musk oxen are being raised on farms in order to increase their numbers, and also to provide the fiber for spinners. Perhaps someday this valuable fleece will become readily available to all spinners. If you are ever able to obtain any, spin it with a loose tension and a fair amount of twist.

Yak

The yak is native to central Asia. The wild Tibetan yak has long, black or brownish-black hair on the chest, legs, flanks, and tail, and it has long, smooth, curving horns. The domestic yak is similar, except that the color varies from white and gray to shades of brown, black, and sometimes red. Yak hair is usually made into rope or woven into cloth. When it is spun, the yarn is somewhat coarse, but attractive. Unspun yak hair is also used as weft for weaving.

Yak hair is available through the larger suppliers of spinning fibers. Dampen or oil it before spinning. It is not difficult to spin, but put in enough twist so that the yarn holds together well and is more durable. You may also wish to blend it with wool.

Highlander

The Highlander, or West Highlander, is native to the mountains and glens of Scotland, and as yet few are raised elsewhere. They are thought to be descendants of the "Kyloe," or "Black cattle," which the Celts drove north and west as they left before the coming of the English.

Highlanders are very hardy and formidable in appearance. They have handsome heads, with wide-spreading horns, and a fine, very thick undercoat covered by long, shaggy hair. The hair is especially long on the forehead, top of the neck, and the thighs. Scottish Highlanders vary in color from yellow to red, brindle, black, or red and black. The small herd raised by a neighbor of mine is made up mainly of red Highlanders.

The thick, soft undercoat of the Highlander as well as the long, outer hair can be spun into very attractive yarn. Add a little oil or oil-and-water mixture prior to spinning.

ANGORA AND OTHER TYPES OF RABBIT FUR

The Angora rabbit, from which we obtain angora yarn, is one of several breeds raised for fur. While Angoras can be clipped, combing or "plucking" is preferred in order to obtain natural fiber ends and greater length. Angora is available in several colors, such as white, gray, chocolate, and black.

Because the fur varies in fineness and length, it really should be sorted and then oiled for ease in handling. Often the angora will need no carding—just a gentle teasing with the fingers.

If you have rather short fiber to spin, use the "spindle in a bowl" method, or loosen the tension on the driving band of your wheel. Practice until you have just the right amount of twist. If you overtwist, your yarn won't be soft, and if you undertwist, the yarn will break easily. If you card the angora with another fiber, such as wool, you'll find the spun yarn quite attractive.

Even the fur from New Zealand rabbits and wild cottontails can be spun in this fashion, with very satisfactory results. Rabbit breeders usually don't mind giving you a sample of rabbit fur now and then. Chinchilla fur can also be spun. If it is very short, blend it with a little wool. The yarn will be very soft to the touch.

OTHER FUR-BEARING ANIMALS

Many other animals—such as raccoons, beavers, muskrats, oppossum, and mink—have soft, downy undercoats suitable for spinning. In most cases, these furs are short-stapled, so their main value to the spinner is as blending fibers, something to card with wool, for example. These animal fibers can be purchased through spinning supply houses, and they are often sorted and cleaned. I usually just add a little oil before carding them.

It's fun to experiment with these fibers, blending them in different amounts. If more wool than fur is used in the blend, the yarn will be rather "wooly" in texture. If more of the fur is used instead, the fiber will have more of the characteristics of fur. If you have access to some unusual fibers, such as bear or kangaroo, try them! I was once given some kangaroo combings, and I carded them with wool. I ended up with a very soft, gray wool-wallaby yarn.

HUMAN HAIR

Yarns made of human hair are strong and durable. They vary from soft and slightly whiskery to downright prickly, depending upon the texture of the hair being used, and how it is spun. These yarns usually have a high luster, and they are expecially attractive when plied or cabled (see page 42). They can also be blended with other types of hair.

Long hair is easiest to spin, but if you can't obtain it, medium-length will do. See if you can't enlist the aid of a hairdresser, so that you'll have a variety of combed and cleaned types to try.

Before spinning, roll the locks of hair in a wet towel until they are just damp. As you spin the hair, smooth down any "whiskers" on the surface of the yarn, wetting them with additional water if necessary. Put in just enough twist to hold the fibers together. When the yarn is spun, skein it, and dip it in a solution of water and hair rinse. When the yarn dries, it will be ready to use.

Braided watchbands, bracelets, rings, necklaces, even bookmarks made of human hair are enjoying a new surge of popularity. If your own hair is long enough, why not make some things as keepsakes for loved ones? Make something for yourself too, such as a hair ornament which can be attached to a bobby pin, or a band or tie to hold your hair back, made of your own hair.

After fashioning an article out of spun hair, snip off any unruly "whiskers" with a scissors. Then spray on a light coating of non-aerosol hair spray, and smooth the surface of the yarn with your fingers.

FIBERS FROM BIRDS

Many birds have been highly prized for their beautiful feathers. Those of the pheasant, the white snowy egret, the peacock, and the ostrich have been used by man to adorn himself for many years. The down of domestic fowl, because of its light weight and fine insulating qualities, has also been used as a filler in bedding, winter coats and vests, and mittens.

Colorful feathers, when removed from the quill and shaft, can be cut up into tiny pieces and carded with wool or other fibers for spinning, as some Indians have done for many years. Small feathers can also be added here and there as you spin another fiber so that the feathers are spaced at intervals along the strand. A yarn such as this is especially effective when woven into a piece containing other natural objects, such as small twigs, grasses, or dried weeds.

Down from fowl such as geese, ducks, and pheasants can also be blended with other fibers. I've spun some very nice blends of wool and down. The yarn is very fluffy and surprisingly soft. It's durable too. This could be another way to make a goosedown vest.

VIII
Spinning Other Fibers

In addition to the animal fibers described in preceeding chapters, there are a number of other fibers which are fun to spin. Among these are the plant fibers, such as cotton, flax, and hemp and the man-made synthetics.

FLAX

Flax, which is used to make linen, has been significant since ancient times because the fibers are strong and smooth, and the linens spun and woven from them are crisp and easy to clean. When the fiber is prepared for spinning, it resembles long, golden hair. The terms "flaxen locks" and "tow-head" are derived from the spinning of this marvelous plant.

In American Colonial times, the powerful English woolen interests made it difficult for the colonists to raise sheep for wool or to improve any sheep they owned by selective breeding. Almost every farmer therefore had his own flax patch, and it was tended with great care. The women of most families spun the flax and then wove their own table and bed linens as well as clothing and other household necessities.

The method of preparing flax stems for spinning was long and arduous. The flax plants were pulled in early July after the blue flowers had been replaced by seed pods. By pulling the plants rather than cutting them, longer stem fibers were obtained. The plants were then cured in the sun. After curing, the pods were removed by "rippling," or drawing the flax stalks through an iron comb.

The next step was "retting" (wetting and rotting). The bundles of stalks were soaked in streams or ponds for a few weeks, or until the fibers became soft, and the leaves were easy to remove. Then the bundles of flax stalks were dried.

In late winter or early spring, the bundles were crushed on a "flax-brake," which was a double, hinged set of boards, usually on legs. The broken stems were then laid on a block of wood and "scutched," or scraped with wooden "swingling-knives." This removed the outer, woody pieces that surrounded the fibers. After scraping, the remaining "strikes," or strands, were tied in bundles, placed either in a trough or on the ground and beaten with a pestle until soft and pliable.

The next procedure was called "hackling," or "hatcheling." Handfuls of dampened fibers were passed through sets of iron teeth inserted in strong, hand-hewn boards called "hatchels," "hackles," or "hacksels." This straightened the fibers and pulled out any remaining short stem pieces, leaving only the long, fine flax fibers. These bunches of golden strands were tied in hanks and later arranged on the distaff of the flax wheel for spinning.

The long hatchel combings were spun and used for fine linens or good clothing. The short hatchel combings, or "tow," were used for rougher cloth and work clothes. With all the time and effort that went into the production of anything made of flax, it is easy to understand why the family linens were so cherished.

After spinning, the skeins were thrown into a "bucking tub," or hollowed-out log. The "bucking," or bleaching, was done with hot water and lye. After washing, the linen was spread in the sun to whiten it further.

Today, most flax is processed by chemical and mechanical means, although in some parts of the world flax growers still prepare flax in the old-fashioned way. They believe that the linen spun from hand-prepared flax is superior to that processed by mechanical methods.

Bleached and unbleached (beige) flax is available in hank form for putting on the distaff of a spinning wheel. Roving is also available, and the fibers can be separated into short, thin slivers or bundles, and spun from the lap. It can also be spun easily on a drop spindle. Flax tow (hackling tow) has a shorter fiber length, and can be dampened and carded into a roving for spinning. Irish flax is a little finer than Belgian flax.

To spin flax top or roving, separate it into thin, manageable lengths about 10″ to 12″ long, and hold in the right hand to spin, using the left hand to smooth out the whiskers that form on the strand. If you keep the flax and the fingers of your left hand moistened, the strand will not be so "hairy."

Flax is very strong and does not require much twisting—just enough to hold the thread together. Keep the bundle of roving, or the rolag, quite thin so that the thread you spin will be slender. Because the flax is spun damp, it will not need to be washed after it has been spun. Just skein it, and when it dries it will be ready to use.

Spinning Flax from the Distaff

A distaff dressed with flax is a thing of beauty: the wheat-colored strands softly criss-crossed with ribbon. It must be done carefully, however, or the flaxen fibers will become hopelessly tangled as you spin. Here's how:

Place the bunch of hackled flax, or strick, on a card or other small table. Take a piece of cord and tie the flax securely near the end closest to you, and tie the cord ends around your waist so that the strick is held secure. (You may wish to pull up a chair and sit for this.) Then, with your left hand, reach out and grasp the opposite end of the flax (the open end), and fan some of it out in a thin layer, moving from left to right. Now, following the accompanying drawings, begin dressing the distaff:

1: Take several strands of the flax from the hank in your left hand and hold them down flat on the table with your right. Begin fanning out another thin layer with the left hand, moving back from right to left.

2: Remove the right hand, and move it next to the left. Transfer the hank of flax to the right hand. Hold down the left edge of the fan with the left hand, and move the right hand back, left to right again, fanning out yet another layer. Continue to do this, crossing back and forth until you have fanned out all the flax. As you work, make certain that the fibers are crossing each other rather than lying side by side. If you are careful about this, the fibers will draw out smoothly for spinning.

3: Untie the cord from your waist, and walk around to the other side of the table so that you face the open end of the fan. Fold up any loose ends into the fan. Place the distaff along the right edge, with the top of the distaff even with the top of the fan. Loosen the tied end of the flax, and begin to wind the fibers around the distaff, rolling from right to left. It should be wound more loosely at the bottom so that the top of the distaff and the once-tied end of the flax stay together.

4: When the flax is wound on the distaff, smooth it a bit, and set the distaff in its holder, or in its place on the wheel, depending upon the type of distaff you have. Take a length of ribbon 2½ yards long or longer, and tie the center around the top of the flax where it had been tied before. Criss-cross the ribbon ends downward several times around the flax until you can tie a knot or bow at the bottom. Fluff up the top of the flax into a smooth tuft so it stands up attractively.

Some spinners prefer to wind some crushed or folded tissue paper around the distaff before winding on the flax. Muslin, cotton flannel, or terry cloth can also be used.

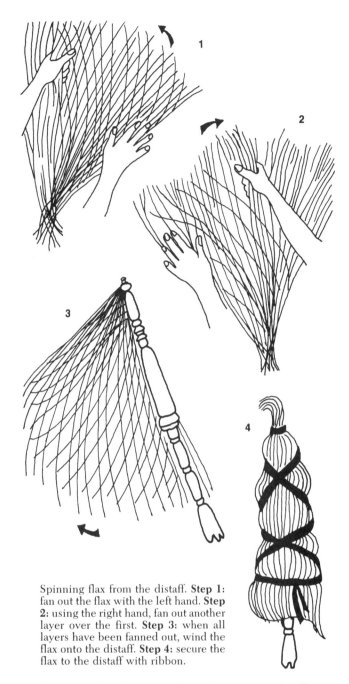

Spinning flax from the distaff. **Step 1:** fan out the flax with the left hand. **Step 2:** using the right hand, fan out another layer over the first. **Step 3:** when all layers have been fanned out, wind the flax onto the distaff. **Step 4:** secure the flax to the distaff with ribbon.

To spin flax from the distaff, position the flax just to the left of you, near the orifice of your wheel. Have a small cup of water near you—perhaps tied on the wheel—to wet your fingers. (You can also moisten your fingers with your own lower lip and tongue.) With the left hand, draw down a few flax fibers from the bottom of the distaff. With a wet thumb and forefinger, join these fibers to the yarn lead, twisting the fibers a bit. Keeping the left hand just a few inches below the bottom of the distaff, begin to treadle slowly.

Allow the flax to draw down continuously through the fingers of the left hand, taking care that the twist doesn't travel up above the hand

When spinning flax, a container of water can be tied to the wheel to moisten the fingers while spinning.

near the distaff. When your fingers become dry, use the right hand momentarily while you again dampen the left. The right hand is also used to smooth the strand, stroking up and away from the wheel, toward the distaff. Remember not to overtwist the flax, and don't hurry. If you're having problems, check the tension on the driving band. It should be fairly loose. You'll need to turn the distaff occasionally, and to retie the ribbon as the flax is gradually used up.

COTTON

From the broad-leafed species of the mallow family (*Gossypium*) we obtain the fiber known as cotton. It has been cultivated by man for thousands of years and in many parts of the world. The plants are from 1½' to 6' tall, and the flowers are usually white, pink, or yellow. These blooms eventually turn red, and when they fall from the plant they are replaced by cotton bolls, sometimes as large as a hen's egg. When the bolls burst, revealing the fleecy cotton, or "lint," they are harvested, and the seeds removed.

There are several types of cotton, such as Egyptian, Peruvian, Sea Island (originally grown on the islands off the coast of the southern United States), and Upland. Some types are finer than others, and they vary in length from less than an inch to about 2½". The Sea Island variety is a favorite of handspinners because it is both fine and long-stapled. Shorter-stapled cottons can be blended with other types and spun. The colors vary from white or cream to yellow, buff, and reddish-brown. The brown cotton is quite lovely, and I enjoy spinning it in combination with other colors and other fibers.

"Middling" cotton is the grade upon which all types are based. Occasionally you'll hear that the cotton is "middling fair," "good middling," "middling," "low middling," or perhaps "ordinary." Usually, when you purchase cotton for handspinning the grades aren't given since those who sell cotton to spinners try to obtain the best grades of cotton available. Cotton can be purchased in roving or sliver form, or as ginned cotton, or even in cotton boll form—in which case you remove the seeds yourself. If you have the right climate and a sunny location, you might enjoy raising your own cotton for spinning.

When you use ginned cotton, check to see if the fiber length varies, and if it does, sort through, making several piles. To "pre-shrink," and to remove dirt and the waxy substance in the cotton, wash it in warm or hot water and soap. You may do so safely because the cotton won't mat. After it is clean and dry, fluff it up with the fingers until it is light and airy. I prefer to card the cotton with cotton carders before spinning, but it can be spun without carding.

Many spinners shy away from cotton because they have heard it is difficult to spin. The short staple length of some types can be a problem, but once you learn to adjust to a shorter, faster draw while spinning, it's really not that difficult. Actually, cotton holds together quite well, and the yarn is highly textured. If you need a very strong yarn, such as for a warp in weaving, blend the cotton with some wool.

To spin cotton on a spindle, set a fairly small, lightweight spindle in a bowl, and twirl it in the bowl as you spin. Because there is no downward pull on the strand, it can be spun very fine. This method has been used for thousands of years.

When using a treadle wheel, put in a little more twist than usual, and loosen the tension on the driving band. As you spin, draw out small amounts of fiber just fast enough to keep ahead of the twist as it travels up the strand.

Chances are that your first few skeins of cotton will be overtwisted. If this is the case, soak them in a little warm water. Then weight them as they dry. As you gain skill, you may still want to wet your skeins, but they won't need to be weighted.

SILK

Long before man began to clothe himself with materials he had spun, nature provided the world with some very skillful little spinners called silkworms. These amazing creatures, only a few inches long, can spin silken threads or filaments as long as two or three thousand feet. The silkworm industry is believed to have originated in China, where silkworms were cultivated by hatching them under controlled conditions and feeding them mulberry leaves.

The silkworm is the caterpillar of the silkworm moth. It spins its marvelous cocoon by means of a spinneret through an opening in the lower lip. Two minute fluid strands, which are spun simultaneously, flow together and, when exposed to the air, harden to form one slender but strong, lustrous thread. It can take as long as four or five days for the little silkworm to spin its cocoon. The cocoons are prevented from hatching by either placing them in hot water, or by steaming them in an oven. The natural gummy substance holding the cocoons together is dissolved, and the silk strands unwound. They are then sorted and washed, and later drawn together, twisted, and reeled in a process called "throwing." This is called reeled silk. The silk is then used in different thicknesses and with differing amounts of twist in the manufacture of various types of cloth.

Not all the silk can be reeled; therefore the manufacture of waste silk, or unreeled silk, is also an industry of some significance. Waste silk is processed further—cleaned, combed, and finally spun into silk yarn for industrial use.

Silk in several forms can be purchased by spinners and weavers. You can buy the cocoons along with instructions for degumming and unwinding, but usually the silk is already degummed. Some spinning supply houses sell cocoon remnants, which can be cut or chopped up, carded and spun into some lovely textured thread. Other sources sell silk sliver (roving), which can be gently separated into lengths which are easy to handle, and then spun into smooth, lustrous thread. Carded silk, or carded silk noil, can also be used to spin some beautiful textured and slubby yarns. My favorite is combed tussah, which comes from various undomesticated Asiatic silkworms. This marvelous, honey-colored fiber is incredibly beautiful, and a joy to spin. Carded tussah, with bits of cocoon in it, can be spun into an interesting thread; however, unlike combed silk, it will not be a smooth strand.

Spinning silk takes a little practice. Use a short draw, and adjust the tension on the driving band until you are able to spin a strong, continuous thread. Practice treadling at different speeds until you find what works best for you. Usually, you'll find that you need to treadle faster.

After spinning and skeining, soak the silk yarn in a lukewarm detergent and water bath, and then rinse. Place the skein in a towel and blot gently. Hang it to dry under light tension.

JUTE

Jute is a smooth, relatively coarse stem fiber that comes from a member of the lime tree group. It is grown extensively in Eastern India and Bangladesh, and it is processed in much the same way as flax. Because the plant grows as high as 12′, the fibers are very long. Jute is one of the least expensive of the vegetable fibers, and it is widely used for coarse yarns, burlap sacks, rug backings, and some types of paper and rugs. It blends well with other fibers although it is not as strong as some other bast types, such as flax.

Jute is rather coarse, and it becomes yellow-brown with age. It is often used, spun or unspun, by weavers, and as cordage by macrame enthusiasts. It can be purchased in roving form, and there is some color choice, from cream-beige to a soft tan. It can be spun on either a spindle or wheel. It's best not to dampen it before spinning or to soak or wash the yarn much after it has been spun. It does have a tendency to rot when kept wet for long periods of time. Simply pull off manageable lengths of the roving, and spin by the worsted method. When jute is woven for industrial use, it is usually given a special finishing treatment to make it more resistant to moisture.

HEMP

The hemp plant belongs to the nettle family, and it may grow as high as 18′ or more under ideal conditions. It is native to Asia, but is now grown in many parts of the world. Hemp is also a stem fiber, and is grown and processed in much the same way as flax. Hemp is somewhat softer and stronger than jute, and it can be bleached and woven. While much of the hemp today is used for cordage and rope, it also makes good carpet warp and cloth.

Hemp roving is easy to spin. Cut the fibers into lengths 10″ or 12″ long, and draw them out into a thin, loose rove, if you are spinning them from your lap. You can also put hemp on the distaff of a treadle wheel. Treat it just as you would flax. Spinning will be easier if the fiber is dampened.

MANILA HEMP

Manila hemp, or abaca, is grown extensively in the Philippines, and is really a member of the plantain or banana family. When flowers appear, the plants are cut. The fibrous outer coating of the leaf stalks are then removed and drawn between a block of wood and a knife with very fine teeth. The pulpy matter is removed, and the remaining long, white fibers are cured, sorted, and baled. These outer leaf fibers are surprisingly strong, and are often used for bags, mats, cord, and binder twine. The finer fibers, however, may be made into clothing. Weavers often find it an interesting fiber because it has both strength and texture.

A spinning wheel works a little better than a spindle for spinning Manila hemp. I find it easiest to cut the fibers into short lengths, as for regular hemp, and lay them across the lap for spinning. Dampening the fiber beforehand will make the spinning easier.

RAMIE

Ramie is another member of the nettle family, and it has been grown as a source of fiber for thousands of years. It is very strong, especially when wet; yet when combed it is almost as soft and fine as silk. The plants grow rapidly and have a high yield. The fibers used for spinning, however, are difficult to remove because they are embedded in a gummy substance between the inner and outer stem coverings of the plant. The lovely, lustrous fiber is obtained only after much scraping, degumming, and boiling-off.

Ramie, also known as China linen, China grass, or rhea, is available in roving form. It has comparatively little elasticity, but does spin up into a soft, lustrous yarn. Ramie can be used for everything from fabric to carpeting, and it is often blended with other fibers. Spin ramie just as you would flax, jute, or hemp.

SISAL

Sisal is a tall tropical plant, with long, pointed leaves that contain a fiber used to make coarse fabric, sacks, and twine or cordage. Sisal is a member of the Agave group, a relative of the amaryllis family. After harvesting, the pulp is cleaned from each side of the leaf, and the remaining fibers are washed and dried in the sun.

Sisal is usually sold in hanks. The fibers may be as long as 4', in which case you'll want to cut them into shorter lengths before spinning. Dampen the sisal by rolling it in a very wet towel for several hours. Then make a slim roving, and smooth the yarn with your free hand so that the yarn is not so "whiskery." Unless the sisal is overtwisted, there will be no need for further wetting.

JAVA COTTON

Java cotton, also known as kapok, is a soft, lustrous fiber obtained from the seed pods of the ceiba tree. It is native to the tropics of the Americas, but is raised extensively in parts of Asia. While the fiber is brittle, it is also silky and water-resistant. Because it keeps its shape so well, it is often used as filling in life preservers, mattresses, and cushions.

While Java cotton is very difficult to spin alone, it can be carded with a support fiber—something with a longer staple, such as grease wool. This will help to hold the shorter fibers in place.

COIR

Coir is obtained from the outer husk of the coconut. The outer husks are customarily removed with a sharpened steel plow point, embedded in a stand. The long fibers are then cleaned, twisted, and used to make cordage for mats and similar articles. Dampen and spin coir as you would sisal.

RAFFIA

The raffia palm is cultivated for its leaves, which are used in thin, dried strips. In some parts of the world, notably Madagascar, raffia is used for sacks, baskets, mats, and various types of outerwear.

Raffia is a coarse fiber, but it is interesting to spin. Dampen it as you would sisal or flax; then divide it into sections and feed the fibers in, a few at a time. Skein the yarn, allow it to dry, and it will be ready to use.

CORN SILKS

Corn silks are very fragile once they are dried; they break easily. They are simply too sticky and tangly to be spun fresh, but if you let them dry partially, and then spin them with a support fiber, such as grease wool, you'll have a satisfactory yarn. I have experimented with corn silk and corresponded with other spinners, among them Delle Gherity, who wrote an article on the subject for *Shuttle, Spindle, and Dyepot* magazine ("The Corn Silk Challenge," Summer, '76). The consensus seems to be that, although "corn silk fallout" is a problem, only the silks on the outer surface shed, while the yarn itself remains strong, even after repeated washings.

I like the idea of using the silks, however fragile they might be, because they add such interest to the yarn. Since the silks are going to break somewhat anyway, it's just as easy to cut the silks into very short lengths and then sprinkle them onto carded wool—or other fiber—just prior to removing the rolag from the carders. The silks shed less when they are embedded in the support fiber before spinning.

MILKWEED FLOSS

Milkweed is widely distributed throughout the tropical and temperate parts of the world. The common milkweed is a plant about 4' or 5' tall. The flowers develop into tapered pods which burst when ripe, exposing the small seeds, each of which has its own white, silky parachute.

Milkweed floss has sometimes been used in place of Java cotton or kapok. Some spinners also prepare the stem fibers as a substitute for flax and hemp.

Although the floss contained in milkweed pods is not difficult to spin, you'll obtain a stronger yarn if you blend it with a support fiber. The seeds are easy to remove: just grasp a bunch of the seeds between the thumb and forefinger of one hand, and pull the silks away. Because the silks tend to float away easily, keep them in a box or bag. Don't wet or oil them; they will stick to the fingers if you do. When you're ready to put some on the carder, reach down into the box or bag and gather a small amount, cupping both hands around them. Roll and pat the silks between the palms to pack them down. If you do this, the fiber can be easily arranged on the carder. Card very lightly—only enough to align the fibers.

For an interesting cream-colored yarn, blend one-third grease wool with two-thirds milkweed floss. Remember to put the wool on the carders first, and brush a few times before putting in the middle layer of short, fine floss. If the yarn isn't strong enough for your purposes, cable several strands together (see page 42), twisting them all into one strand in the same direction they were spun the first time.

Another way to achieve an interesting yarn is to card a thin roving of milkweed floss and, as you spin some wool, lay in the loose roll of milkweed fiber all along the surface of the woolen yarn. This takes time, but the yarn is beautiful. After washing thoroughly, it will be a creamy white, with a glossy finish. Shake the wet skein to fluff it, and don't weight it heavily.

Swamp milkweed (*Asclepias incarnata*) is a perennial herb that has rounded, reddish flower heads in the summertime. The seed pods contain floss and seeds much like those of the common milkweed, except that the seed hairs are somewhat shorter. I gather the pods each autumn so that I can card the floss with wool, mohair, silk, and other fibers.

DANDELION FLUFF

Dandelion fluff can be carded with wool, or other fibers, seeds and all. The yarn is soft, textured, and reasonably strong. Handle as you would milkweed floss. This fiber is somewhat messy to handle, but fun nonetheless.

CATTAIL FLUFF

When I was a child, a wise old Indian, who was known for his interest in plant foods and medicines, handed me a cattail spike and told me that this was indeed a wondrous and useful plant. The young shoots of the cattail, he said, could be prepared and eaten as a vegetable; the pollen was inflammable, so the plant could be used as a torch; and, he added, both the brown flower heads and the fluff which burst from them could be used for adornment.

The cattail, sometimes called the bulrush, grows in marshy areas. Its most prominent feature is its cinnamon-brown flower, perched atop a long stem. The leaves are long, slender, and graceful. When the cattail flowers finally burst, releasing the white seed hair, this fluffy fiber can be collected and used as a blending fiber for spinning.

To obtain a textured, soft beige yarn, card two parts cattail fluff with one part wool. The yarn will be fluffy, with tiny bits of brown throughout. For a beautiful tan yarn, card the fluff with an equal amount of flax tow.

Remember that cattail fluff, like most blending fibers, is not very strong by itself, so you must choose a strong support fiber. The cattail yarns hold up very well after washing even though there is some shedding from the surface of the yarn.

THISTLE DOWN

The short, glistening seed hairs of the thistle plant may seem a strange fiber to spin, but they really do add a nice texture to yarn. Try carding two parts thistle down with one part grease wool for a soft, yet sparkly thread.

COTTONWOOD FLUFF

The cottonwood tree is well-known for its white, short-stapled fluff, which covers lawns and streets in early summer. This, too, is a good blending fiber to use when you want yarn with an interesting texture. If you set the tension on the driving band so that it is quite slack, it is possible to spin pure cottonwood fluff, but for a more durable yarn, blend the fluff with a support fiber. Gray or black grease wool with cottonwood fluff added results in a very striking yarn.

SYNTHETIC FIBERS

Man-made fibers, especially the acrylics, nylons, and polyesters, can be obtained in roving or sliver form, and often in a variety of colors. Acrylics, such as orlon, are soft, quick-drying, and moth- and wrinkle-resistant. Nylon is lustrous, elastic, and dries quickly. Polyesters are durable, wash easily, shrink very little, and keep their shape well. While I prefer natural fibers, there are times when I do blend synthetics with natural ones. I seldom spin pure man-mades because I simply don't find them as pleasant to use.

Synthetics are clean when you purchase them, and they do not need sorting. Some spinners prefer to add oil before spinning; some do not. If in roving form, the fiber can be pulled off in thin bunches and spun, or else carded with hand carders to prepare them for woolen spinning.

If you cannot obtain the synthetic fiber you want from a spinning supply house, you might try writing to mills that use them. Synthetic fiber for stuffing pillows can also be used, providing the staple is long enough.

Remember to handle man-mades gently, just as you would natural fibers, especially when washing the yarn. If you are allergic to some of the natural fibers, perhaps synthetics are for you.

IX

Making Novelty Yarns

Have you ever spent time in a shop that sells handspun yarns, gazing at extraordinary colors and blends, running your fingers over the irregularities and textures that make them unique and so appealing? You can spin lovely and unusual yarns yourself, just as spinners have been doing for years. Why not try your hand at creating variegated or marbled ones, soft heathers, nubby blends, or "thick-and-thin" yarns? Most of these are more easily made on a wheel, where you have both hands free to work, but some can be made just as easily on a spindle.

Fancy plied yarns. Some very attractive yarns can be made by plying strands with different types of twists. (See page 26 for instructions on how to ply.) Try combining an S-twisted yarn and a Z-twisted yarn with an S-twist. Watch one become twisted more tightly, while the other becomes loose and fluffy. Or, ply two Z-twisted yarns—one very thick and loose, the other thin and tightly spun—with an S-twist. Watch the character of the yarns change as they are plied. The results can be very exciting, and the possibilities are endless.

Ply yarns made of different fibers, such as mohair and dog hair. This is great fun! Just be sure that the yarns have about the same amount of elasticity and durability, and that they will shrink at about the same rate when washed.

Plying several single yarns of different colors can give you some very eye-catching results. Someone once brought me a bag of Chow combings and asked me to make an earwarmer or skiband from it. I found quite a variety of colors among the combings, mainly reds and grays. I made one yarn in various shades of red and cream and another in different shades of gray. Then the two were plied, and the result was a lovely variegated yarn. The skiband was made of this red-gray combination, edged with a deep charcoal Chow yarn for contrast.

Many spinners enjoy dyeing fibers or yarns with natural or synthetic dyes. If you become interested in this fascinating hobby, you'll have quite a variety of colors to use. You might even want to ply three different yarns, such as a brown-orange-gold combination, or perhaps a dark green-medium green-white three-ply yarn. These have great eye-appeal. Try it.

Varying the tension can also produce some interesting results. If you are plying a black and a gray yarn, for example, hold back the gray for a second, then quickly push it ahead so that it wraps unevenly around the black yarn. Continue to do this so that the plying is purposely and regularly uneven. You can do the same thing with yarns of the same color that differ in texture.

Would you like to change the character of some left-over or unused commercially produced yarn? Combine it with one of your homespuns, or cut it into 2″ or 3″ lengths and insert the pieces as you spin some yarns of your own.

Cabling. Cabled yarns are those which are respun in the same direction in which they were originally twisted, as when two Z-twisted yarns are again spun together with a Z-twist. The resulting yarn is shorter, firmer, and more lustrous, since the twist is intensified as you spin them again in the same direction.

Cabled yarns can be effectively combined with plied yarns and singles in weaving. If a lustrous fiber is used—such as mohair or human hair—the cabled yarn will be very glossy and quite attractive.

Slub yarns. As any spinning novice knows, slubs are lumps in the yarn. It is not difficult to draw thick lumps when you are learning to spin, but to regulate the placement of these slubs so that the yarn still has uniformity requires some skill. First, learn to spin an even strand, and then practice incorporating slubs where you want them in your yarn.

To make a slub, just draw a larger mass of fiber out from the rolag. If the fiber has a short staple length, make a shorter slub; if the fiber has a long staple length, you can make the slubs longer also. Space them closely, or far apart, just so long as the slubs are not too large to pass around the hooks of the flyer on your wheel.

Carded fiber blends. Fibers can be combined by carding them together before spinning. One very nice blend is half wool and half combed chinchilla fur (or three-fourths wool and one-fourth chinchilla). It's fun to experiment. If you use more wool, the yarn will be more "wooly," and if you use more fur, the yarn will have more of the properties of fur.

There are several ways to combine fibers. This is my favorite method. Let's say that you want to blend some wool with some short, but very soft collie combings ("puppy fuzz," for instance). Place the longer fiber on the left-hand card first—in this case, the wool—and comb through a few times with the right-hand card to distribute the wool evenly on the cards. Then place the desired amount of collie combings over the wool on the left-hand card. Draw the right-hand card over again, carding in the usual way, until the two fibers are blended. Then remove the batt, forming a rolag.

Try to card the same proportion of wool to collie each time. Uneven blending is sometimes done intentionally, but unless care is taken very noticeable irregularities show up in the finished yarn—ones that may not have been wanted.

Don't forget some of the more unusual novelty fibers, many of which you can gather yourself. Card small amounts of such things as milkweed silks, goose down, cattail fluff, or thistledown with a support fiber such as wool, or even flax tow or cotton, depending on how the yarn will be used.

Long, combed fibers of differing textures can also be blended by combining them as you spin, using two rolags at a time. You can draw them at the same time or alternately.

Carded color blends. Some of the loveliest yarns of all are those that are a subtle blending of several colors, but in which each color can still be distinguished from the rest. Any number of colors can be used.

To blend colors, first spread one color on the left-hand card and lightly comb through it one or two times with the other card. Then spread on strips of another color, in the amount desired, on the left-hand card. Comb through again. Continue this until all colors have been added, and until they are well blended. Then strip the cards and form the rolag. If the fibers vary in length, try to put the longer fibers on the carders first. I usually blend from two to five colors. I find that the drum carding machine is wonderful for blending colors. First put on one color; then add others, one at a time.

Try to keep the proportion of each color the same in each rolag. You can blend the colors until they are very well mixed, or you can blend them only partially. If the colors remain somewhat separated, you will have a marbled effect when the rolag is spun.

Before spinning large amounts of marbled or variegated yarns, knit, crochet, or weave a sample swatch to be certain that you will get the desired effect. You may find that the finished product will have a better appearance if you card the fiber a bit differently.

Longer, combed fibers can easily be used to make streaked or marbled yarns by making two different-colored rolags and combining them during the spinning process. You can also produce "ombre" yarns by spinning. Spin a short length of one color; join on another colored rolag and spin that one; join on another, and so forth, continuing to add on each color in its proper order. (For example: brown-rust-gold; brown-rust-gold.)

"**Nubby**" **yarns.** Yarns with little bits, or "nubs," of contrasting colors spaced here and there are very pretty. Don't use pieces of your better yarns for this. Just cut up bits of left-over yarns or chunks of unspun fibers. The short bits of wool left after sorting a fleece are nice for this, or use small amounts of very short fur.

To make a "nubby" yarn, card a support fiber such as wool, and just before removing it from the carding combs, sprinkle on some tiny bits of yarn or fiber. Put them on liberally, and use several colors, if you wish. Then comb through them a few times, just enough to embed the little pieces in the wool, but not so much that they become mixed in. Strip the cards in the usual manner, and form the rolag. Care should be taken to make sure that the tiny pieces are somewhat evenly distributed throughout the rolag. It's also a good idea to keep some additional bits handy while you spin, in case you need to add a few more in certain places.

Some spinners prefer to add the tiny pieces during the spinning of the wool, although they fall out more easily when this is done. It's also more time-consuming to add the pieces by this method.

A friend of mine, now in her seventies, has often made yarns of this type. This is her method:

> Take an old sweater or cap that has outlived its usefulness, and cut it up into little pieces. Simmer the dickens out of them in a kettle of soapy water. Then rinse, and let them dry. Card the little pieces of yarn with some white, gray, or other colored wool, and you'll end up with a very pretty speckled yarn.

The idea of using an old sweater, cap, or other worn-out item is especially appealing today when recycling is so important.

Poodle fanciers might enjoy making this nubby yarn, using poodle hair. Card some long wool, and just before removing the fiber, sprinkle on some short, tightly curled wisps of poodle hair. Draw the right-hand card lightly through the left, just enough to embed the short curls in the wool, but not enough to lose the unusual texture of the tiny curled pieces. Then strip the cards and remove the rolag in the usual way. There will be little wisps of hair all through the yarn. This will produce a yarn that is especially nice for weaving, or perhaps to trim a wooly, knitted cap.

Recarding spun yarn. If you have some yarn that is unsatisfactory because it was carelessly blended or poorly spun, don't throw it away. Spin it over again. Cut it into short lengths, dampen it, and card it. You may need to card it several times to break the old yarn down to the "bits and pieces" stage.

If you want an unusual texture, spin the recarded yarn with some of the lengths of old yarn still remaining, or break down the old yarn completely, and spin it again.

X
Using Your Homespun Yarns

Now that you have spun your yarn, you will want to use it to make something special. Homespun yarns can be used for all of the projects for which you would use a commercially spun yarn: weaving, knitting, crocheting, embroidery, macrame, etc. The same basic instructions apply to all yarns. Here are a few suggestions, however, to help make your projects easier and more satisfactory.

When planning your project, always keep the type of yarn in mind. A soft wool or a mohair yarn is perfect for baby booties, or for something worn close to your skin, such as a sweater or scarf. Silk, linen and cotton are wonderful for woven placemats, scarves, or yard goods. A medium or slightly coarse worsted yarn is fine for items that must be durable, such as slippers, mittens and rugs. Use a very coarse, hairy yarn in a way that will show off its texture to advantage—perhaps in a shoulder bag or wall hanging. Remember that woolen yarns are usually softer and fluffier than worsteds; plied yarns are more durable than singles.

Use your novelty yarns to the best advantage. One of the most beautiful and unusual purses I have ever seen was a crocheted shoulder bag made of human hair yarn in an auburn shade. Yarn from pet dogs and cats can be braided and fashioned into leashes and collars. One especially nice collar was worn proudly by a handsome, large, grey Angora cat. It was, of course, made of his own fur, carded with a little gray wool. His owner had braided it with some nylon fishing line to give the collar added strength. Why not knit your poodle an overcoat made of yarn spun from his own coat? I once made a lovely cap and mitten set from buffalo wool. A spinner from Australia wrote that she saw a very attractive man's cap on display at an arts and crafts exhibition in Sydney; it was made of German shepherd combings. A spinner from California sent me a photograph of a lovely striped vest she had made using keeshond, Afghan hound and Norwegian elkhound combings. My samoyed, Frosty, has supplied me with enough fur to knit a poncho.

WEAVING

Both woolen and worsted yarns can be used as weft. You can also use unspun fiber, but if you do, it should have a fairly long staple. Woven materials which have unspun fiber as weft should never be put under too much tension.

A homespun single-ply warp can make a durable woven material which is often very lightweight. When spinning warp, choose a durable fiber with a long staple. Prepare and spin it by the worsted method, so you will have a strong, smooth yarn. Keep the yarn as uniform as possible. It should be somewhat overspun to give it extra strength, and then allowed to set on a bobbin, or in a ball, for a few days. Then it should be spun in reverse and again allowed to set.

Some weavers feel there is no need for a warp dressing, while others say it is a "must." If you like to use one, try skim milk, plastic starch, or commercial sizing.

Don't forget to use yarns with slubs and fancy twists. When combining both fine and coarse types, try to keep a balance so you avoid distortion.

KNITTING AND CROCHETING

In working a knit or crochet pattern, stitch gauge is important. Since your own homespun yarns will not always be the same, in size and weight, as those purchased in a store, you'll have to experiment a little. It's a good idea to make a few 3″ swatches before you start to determine what size needles or crochet hook to use. If you watch your gauge carefully as you work, you'll have no trouble at all using your homespun yarns to make any of your favorite projects.

After finishing each piece of work, only a light steaming will be necessary. A steam iron works best for this. Don't allow the iron to rest on the fabric. If the garment does need additional blocking to reshape it a little, you will need a padded, flat surface and some rust-proof pins. Steam the pieces, shape them, and pin them down on the padded surface, using plenty of pins. Let the pieces dry thoroughly.

Some fibers have a tendency to stretch with wear and repeated washings. To help knitted or crocheted articles keep their shape, run some thin elastic thread through wherever a close fit is required, especially along ribbings. If this is done carefully, with a large needle, it will not be noticeable from the outside, and it will insure a neat, comfortable fit.

When you first start knitting or crocheting with your yarns, practice on small pieces—a child's cap and mittens, slippers, a vest or a sweater for a toddler. When you begin a piece of work, start with the end of the yarn you spun first. If you do this the article you make will keep its new appearance longer.

NEEDLEPOINT AND EMBROIDERY

For most needlepoint projects, choose an even, fairly thin yarn. It may be plied, if you wish, for added strength. Because the yarn will be subjected to much wear as it is drawn through the canvas, select a firm one—preferably a worsted—with quite a bit of twist. A worsted yarn will not "fuzz up" as much either.

For creative stitchery, you can use just about any type of yarn to add variety and interest to your work. Try loosely twisted and lumpy ones, or shiny, smooth ones. Unusually plied yarns are very effective. Concentrate on variety in both color and texture. When working on a very fine fabric, use gossamer-fine homespun—perhaps cotton or silk thread, with touches of linen here and there.

MACRAMÉ

For macramé, the yarn you use should be spun by the worsted method. It should have a fair amount of twist so that it is firm, smooth, and durable. This is important because the yarn is handled so much during the knotting.

Save your coarser, longer fibers for your macramé projects. Experiment with different textures and colors. Jute and jute blends are very nice for macramé, and so are hemp and sisal. Just be sure you use a strong fiber. Some types of pet hair make good macramé cordage.

Bibliography and Sources of Supply

BOOKS ON SHEEP AND TYPES OF WOOL

Jones, G., *Breeds of Sheep*. Available through the author, Jones Sheep Farm, Rt. 2, Box 185D, Peabody, Kansas 66866.

British Wool Marketing Board, *British Sheep Breeds, Their Wool, and Its Uses*, published through the British Wool Marketing Board. Available from Straw Into Gold. 3006 San Pablo Ave., Berkeley, California 94702. Also through other sources.

Sheep! Magazine, Dept. 6, Waterloo, Wisconsin 53594. An excellent new periodical on sheep raising, spinning and related subjects.

Simmons, *Sheep Raising the Modern Way*. Available from Handcraft Wools Ltd., Box 378, Streetsville, Ontario, Canada L5M 2B9. Also through other sources. Written by a wool craftsperson. Good.

Teller, *Starting Right with Sheep*, Available from Straw Into Gold. 3006 San Pablo Ave., Berkeley, California 94702. Also through other sources.

BOOKS ON SPINNING WHEELS

Pennington, David and Michael Taylor. *A Pictorial Guide to American Spinning Wheels*. Available through The Penningtons, 1993 W. Liberty, Ann Arbor, Michigan 48103. Excellent. A "must" for anyone who collects or restores old spinning wheels.

Thompson, G., *Spinning Wheels*, Ulster Museum, Belfast, Ireland: the John Horner Collection. Several spinning supply houses, such as Straw Into Gold, and Handcraft Wools, have this one in stock.

PLANS FOR MAKING SPINNING WHEELS

Antique and Woodcrafts, Box 32, Kapushasing, Ontario, Canada: A treadle type reproduction. Eight pages of plans.

Council for Small Industries in Rural Areas, 141 Castle Street, Salisbury, Wilts., SP13TP England: Two Saxony types. Ask for plans numbers 23 and 25.

Earthwares, 103 N. Pleasant St., Amherst, Massachusetts 01002: Plans for a Saxony wheel and for a Lazy Kate.

Gordon's Naturals, P.O. Box 506. Roseburg, Oregon 97470: Several sets of spinning wheel plans, such as the "Kliot Walker," which uses a bicycle wheel (a wool wheel), and a book, *Anyone Can Build a Spinning Wheel*, by W. C. West are listed in their general catalog under "Spinning Supplies."

Workbench Magazine, 4251 Pennsylvania, Kansas City, Missouri 64111: Nice plans for a parlor, or upright, wheel.

SPINNING SUPPLIES AND SERVICES

Albion Hills Farm School, R. R. 3, Caledon East, Ontario, Canada, Spinning workshops and supplies.

Ashford Handicrafts, Ltd., P.O. Box 474, Ashburton, New Zealand: High quality spinning wheels for beginners to experts. Accessories including hand and drum cards and selected New Zealand wools. Free catalog.

D. Bailey, 15 Dutton St., New South Wales, Australia: Fibers and natural dyes.

Bonneville Gallery of Weaving, 3102 Harborview Dr., Gig Harbor, Washington 98335: Classes, books, spinning and weaving supplies

Clemes & Clemes,, Inc., 650 San Pablo Ave., Pinole, California 94564.

Clara Creager, 75 W. College Ave., Westerville, Ohio 43081: Books and spinning equipment.

Creager Tools for the Crafts, 40 W. College Ave., Westerville, Ohio 43081: Antique spinning wheels and tools, new wheels, spinning fibers.

Dryad, P.O. Box 38, Northgates, Leicester, LE19BU United Kingdom: Spinning fibers.

Fallbrook House, R.D. 2, Box 17, Troy, Pennsylvania 16947: Excellent line of spinning and dyeing supplies. Even cotton carders. A great variety of novely spinning fibers.

Fibre Crafts, 38 Center St., Clinton, New Jersey 08809: Supplies for spinning, books, lessons.

Fricke Enterprises, 8702 State Rd., 92, Granite Falls, Washington 98252: Wool carding machines and hand carders. Replacement card cloth for Fricke machines.

Frye's Measure Mill, Wilton, New Hampshire 03086: Several types of carders, and flicker combs. Also replacement facings (cloth) for some of their carders.

Gordon's Naturals, P.O. Box 506, Roseburg, Oregon 97490: Excellent source for all materials related to spinning and dyeing.

Greentree Ranch Wools, 163 N. Carter Lake Rd., Loveland, Colorado 80537: Fibers for spinning, and equipment of all types. Their wheels and spindle are very nice.

Guild of Shaker Crafts, Spring Lake, Michigan 49456: Shaker wheels, niddy-noodies, other spinning supplies.

Handcraft Wools, Ltd., Box 378, Streetsville, Ontario L5M2B9, Canada: Full line of spinning supplies.

Howard Bros. Manufacturing Co., 42 Southbridge St., Auburn, Massachusetts 01501: Carders, including cotton carders.

Jones Sheep Farm, Route 2, Box 185D, Peabody, Kansas 66866: A very complete line of wool for spinning, including Karakul. Also sells mohair.

Joseph's Coat, 131 W. Main, Missoula, Montana 59801: Books, supplies.

Joyous Song, 10109 Farmington Dr., Fairfax, Virginia 22030: Lovely and unusual drop spindles. A little more expensive, but worth it.

M. W. Klein, 1053 Blue Heron Dr., Sanibel, Florida 33957: Stoneware spindle whorls.

Eliza Leadbeater, Rookery Cottage, Whitegate, Northwich, Chesire CW8 2BN, England: Unusual fibers for spinning. Also dye materials.

Made-well Manufacturing Co., Box 22, Sifton, Manitoba, Canada: Spinning wheels. Cotton carders. Cylinder carding machines.

The Mannings, P.O. Box 687, East Berlin, Pennsylvania 17316: Spinning dyeing and weaving supplies.

Marvin Mueller, 421 E. North St., Jefferson, Wisconsin 53549: Wheel repair. Also other spinning tools, such as drop spindles and niddy-noddies.

I. Nagy, P.O. Box 9637, Wellington, New Zealand: Spinning wheels of high quality.

Nasco, 901 Janesville Ave., Fort Atkinson, Wisconsin 53538 (or) **Nasco,** 1524 Princeton Ave., Modesto, California 95352: Their crafts catalog lists spinning and weaving supplies. Also books on crafts.

The Hidden Village, 4650 Arrow Highway, #G2, Montclair, California 91763: A good line of spinning wheels, reasonable prices.

The Niddy Noddy, One Croton Point Ave., Croton-on-Hudson, New York 10520: Spinning fibers and equipment.

Orchard House Weavers, Rt. 14, Windham Center, Connecticut 06280: Weaving and spinning supplies, Lessons, SASE.

Pendleton Shop, 465 Jordan Rd., Box 233, Sedona, Arizona 86336: Retail store, also classes in spinning and weaving.

The Penningtons, 1993 W. Liberty, Ann Arbor, Michigan 48103: Spinning and dyeing materials. Books and lessons. A variety of fibers.

River Farm, Rt. 1, P.O. #169A. Timberville, Virginia 22853: Black, brown and gray fleeces. Spinning workshops.

Riverside Acres, Kathy Kelnhofer, Rt. 1, Box 143, Rice Lake, Wisconsin 54868: She raises her own Angora rabbit fur for spinning. Available by the ounce, in a variety of colors.

C. Rognvaldson, 265 Main St., N., Acton, Ontario, Canada: Wheel restoration.

Serendipity Shop, 2 Prairie St., Park Ridge, Illinois 60068: Spinning and weaving supplies. Books.

Sievers Looms and Schools, Washington Island, Wisconsin 54246: Classes in spinning, dyeing and textile designs.

Silver Shuttle, 1301 35th St. N. W., Washington, D.C. 20007: Spinning and weaving supplies.

Paula Simmons, 48793 Chilliwak Lake Road, Sardis, British Columbia V2R 2P1 Canada: Spinning oil, and warp sizing for weavers who spin their own warp. Written material on spinning and weaving. Yarn spun to order.

The Spinning Room, 3767 Sulphur Springs Rd., Toledo, Ohio 43606: Books and supplies.

Spin n' Weave, 3054 North First Ave., Tucson, Arizona 85719: Books, supplies, group and private instructions.

Stevens, Lindgård RR 2, Barnesville, Minnesota 56514: Scottish Blackface and other types of fleece for spinning. Also spinning wheels.

Straw Into Gold, 3006 San Pablo Avenue, Berkeley, California 94702: A very complete source for spinning supplies. Spinning books, cotton carders, hard-to-obtain fibers, such as jute and muskrat fur.

Traditional Handcrafts, 154 Mary Alexander Court, Northville, Michigan 48167: Very good source of spinning and dyeing supplies, weaving, knitting.

Valley Fibres, Ltd., 401 Richmond Rd., Ottawa, Canada K2A OE9: Books, supplies, equipment.

Village Wools, 308 San Gelipe, N. W., Albuquerque, New Mexico 87104: Spinning supplies.

The Weaver's Shop, 39 Courtland, Rockford, Michigan 49341: Spinning supplies, classes and summer workshops.

Weaving Workshop, 817½ E. Johnston St., Madison, Wisconsin 53703: Wool, spinning wheels and other supplies for spinners.

J. H. Wilson, 44 Minter St., Canterbury, New South Wales, Australia: Spinning and weaving supplies, including wheels.

The Wool-N-Shop, North Central Wool Marketing, 101 27th Ave., S.E., Minneapolis, Minnesota 55414: A variety of fibers for spinning.

Wooltique, 1111 Elm Grove St., P.O. Box 537, Elm Grove, Wisconsin 53122: Nature spun yarns and wool combed top. Spinning wheels and accessories.